# Summer Fit Activities™

## Fourth to Fifth Grade

# Build Fit Brains and Fit Bodies!

 Fun, skill-based activities in reading, writing, mathematics, and language arts with additional activities in science and geography. Curriculum activities are based on national standards.

 Summer Fitness program includes aerobic and strength exercises. Fitness log, exercise videos and instructions included. Keeping young bodies active and strong helps children live better, learn more and feel healthier.

 Incentive Contract Calendars motivate children to complete activities and exercises by rewarding their efforts. Summer Explorers are lists of fun and active things to do — perfect for when your child says, "I'm bored, what can I do?"

 Core values and role model activities include child activities, parent talking points and reading lists.

 Summer Journaling, Book Reports, Health and Nutrition Index, Certificate of Completion and Flashcards.

Access more summer resource materials at
**www.SummerFitActivities.com**

# 3rd Edition

Written by: Kelly Terrill and Sarria James

Fitness and Nutrition: Lisa Roberts RN, BSN, PHN, Coach James Cordova and Charles Miller

Cover Design: Andy Carlson

For orders or product information call 801-466-4272

## Dedication

Summer Fit™ is dedicated to Julia Hobbs and Carla Fisher who are the original authors of Summer Bridge Activities™. Julia and Carla helped pioneer summer learning and dedicated their lives to their vocation of teaching.

## Caution

Exercises may require adult supervision. If you have any concerns regarding your child's ability to complete any of the suggested fitness activities, consult your family doctor or pediatrician. Children should always stretch and warm up before exercises. Do not push children past comfort level or ability. Exercises were created to be fun for parents and caregivers as well as the child, but not as a professional training or weight loss program. Exercise should stop immediately if you or your child experiences any of the following symptoms: pain, feeling dizzy or faint, nausea, or severe fatigue.

## Copyright

ISBN  978-0-9762800-0-2

# Table of Contents

Online Password:
## ORANGE45

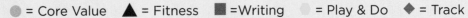

★ = Academic  ● = Core Value  ▲ = Fitness  ■ =Writing  ○ = Play & Do  ◆ = Track

# Dear Parents,

Thank you for choosing **Summer Fit Activities**™ to help reinforce your child's classroom skills while away from school. Summer Fit™ is a fun and motivational way to keep your child active and learning during a very important time in your child's life – summer vacation.

We believe in summer vacation and all the magical experiences that children grow from during this fun and carefree time. Summer vacation is important for both personal and family growth. Many life-long memories come from this time of the year.

Your personal involvement with your child's education is vitally important to their immediate and long-term success. Summer is a great opportunity to reinforce classroom skills and lifestyle habits.

**Summer Fit Activities**™ is a result of over 20 years of experience in summer learning workbooks and educational resources. It contains what we believe are the three foundation pieces of success: academics, health and character education. Summer Fit™ is easy to use and makes summer learning fun. It is self-motivating and effective in getting your child ready for the new school year at home, on the road or at grandma's house.

Thank you again for choosing **Summer Fit Activities**™ to assist your child's academic success and personal growth. We do offer additional fun activities, ideas and games online at **www.SummerFitActivities.com**. Use your grade appropriate password found on the Table of Contents page to register to receive seasonal activities throughout the year. We look forward to seeing you there!

Have a wonderful, fun-filled, active summer!

Sincerely,

Summer Fit Activities™

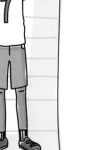

# INSIDE
# Summer Fit Activities™

Here is what you will find inside Summer Fit™:

## Academics

- There are 5 sections of academic exercises, each section with its own core value and journal entry page.

- Sections begin with Incentive Contract Calendars and "Summer Explorer" activity lists.

- Your child will complete activities in reading, writing, math and language arts. Science and geography activities are included throughout the book.

- When your child completes each day, he/she may color or initial the academic and reading icon for that day on the Incentive Contract Calendar.

- Parents initial the Incentive Contract Calendar once the section has been completed.

## Fitness

Research shows that keeping bodies strong and healthy helps children learn better, live better and even miss fewer days of school! To keep bodies healthy, children need to eat right, get enough sleep and exercise daily.

- The Summer Fitness Program helps children set goals and track performance over the summer.

- Includes aerobic and strength exercises.

- Fitness & Health Index includes Nutrition page, Foods to Eat Everyday & Meal Tracker.

- Online videos show the proper way to complete exercises.

## Character Education

Core values are fundamental to society and are incorporated into our civil laws. Research shows that character education is more effective when parents encourage values in their child's daily routine. Core values are vitally important to the overall growth, well-being and success of all children.

- Each section highlights two different values and role models.

- Value activities are designed for children and parents.

- Each value includes a reading comprehension activity based on role models from throughout the world.

# Helpful Hints for Summer Fit™

**1** Flip through the book to become familiar with the layout and activities. Look ahead to the upcoming core value so you can incorporate discussions and activities into your daily routine.

**2** Provide your child with the tools he/she will need to complete the work: pencils, pens, crayons, ruler and a healthy dose of encouragement.

**3** Try to set aside a specific time to do Summer Fit™ each day (for example, after breakfast each morning). Make sure your child has enough time to complete the day's work and exercise.

**4** Be a cheerleader! Encourage your children to do their best, urging them to challenge themselves. Make sure they know you are there to help them if they need support. Talk about and reinforce the material in the book beyond the page. For example, after reading about insects, encourage your child to find an insect in the yard to observe and draw.

**5** Look at your child's work frequently. Make sure they know you value what they are doing and that it is not just "busywork."

**6** Try doing Summer Fit™ outside in the fresh air. At the park, in the backyard, camping, or on the beach — Summer Fit™ can go wherever you go!

**7** Ask older siblings, grandparents, babysitters and even friends to participate in and give one-on-one help with the activities. Summer Fit™ is a great shared experience!

**8** Keep up with the Incentive Contract Calendars. Follow through and reward completed work. Stamps, stickers, hugs and high fives are great ways to motivate and recognize a job well done.

**9** Let your child do more than one page at a sitting if he/she is enthusiastic and wants to work ahead. Make sure to check the website for additional activities and resources that can help you tailor Summer Fit™ to your child's needs.

**10** When the book has been completed, display the Certificate of Completion proudly and let your child know what a great job he/she did. Celebrate!

# Encourage Summer Reading and Writing

Reading and writing skills are important skills for your child's success. Summer is a great time to encourage and build reading and writing skills with your child regardless of ability.

You can do many things to encourage literacy and writing:

 Make Reading a Priority: Create a routine by establishing a reading time each day for your child.

 Read Around Your Child: Read in front of him/her as much as possible. Talk with your child about the books you are reading.

 Create a Summer Reading List: Find books that involve your child's favorite interests like sports, art, mysteries, dance, etc.

 Reading On The Road: Billboards, menus, street signs, window banners and packaging labels are great ways to reinforce reading comprehension skills.

 Storytelling: Have campfire nights in your backyard and tell stories about things you did when you were their age. Slip in a few scary spooks as well!

 Read Together: Newspapers, magazine articles and stories on the Internet are great to read together and discuss.

 Library Time: Go to the library on a weekly basis to choose new books.

 Letter Writing: Encourage your child to write thank you notes and letters.

 Plan a Trip: Have your child plan a trip for the family. Have him/her write an overview of the trip including where, what to bring, how to travel, how long and what you will do on your trip.

 Create a Joke Book: Provide a list of subjects for your child to create jokes about.

 Family Writing Hour: Sit down as a family and write a story together. Read the story out loud at the end.

 Script Writing: Ask your child to write a movie script. When it is finished, perform it as a family – be sure to video the production!

 Poetry: Discuss different forms of poetry. Have your child write a poem. Add an illustration.

# Parents are Key to Summer Learning

Many parents believe the academic success of their child is based largely on their child's natural abilities rather than parent involvement. However, research shows parent involvement has a significant impact on student behavior, student academic performance and student quality of life.

This summer you are investing in the overall development of your child by engaging them academically, physically and socially by establishing values that are important to you and your family.

Encourage your children to build their skills and abilities in all areas of their life by participating with them as they complete their activities and exercises. As a parent you are often the biggest influence on your child's life. Patience, understanding and encouragement are key qualities that you as a parent bring into your child's development by being present and involved.

# 5 Parent Tips

 **Routine** Set a time and a place for your child to complete their activities and exercises each day.

 **Balance** Use a combination of resources to reinforce basic skills in fun ways. Integrate technology with traditional learning, but do not replace one with another.

 **Motivate and Encourage** Inspire your child to complete his/her daily activities and exercise. Get excited and show your support for his/her accomplishments!

 **Play as a Family** Slap "High 5," jump up and down and get silly! Show how fun it is to be active and playing by doing it yourself. Health experts recommend 60 minutes of play a day, and kids love seeing parents playing and having fun!

 **Eat Healthy and Together** Children are more likely to eat less healthy during the summer than during the school year. Serve lots of fruits and vegetables and have dinner together as a family.

# Living Earth Friendly

We all share this home called Earth, and each one of us needs to be responsible in helping take care of her. There are many things families can do together to REDUCE, REUSE, and RECYCLE in order to be kind to Mother Earth. We can all BE SMART AND DO OUR PART!

There are many opportunities each day for us to practice these little steps with our children and we should talk with them about how little things add up to make a big impact.

# REDUCE, REUSE, RECYCLE

**REDUCE:** Means to use less of something. Encourage your children to use water wisely, turn off lights when leaving a room, and use your own bags at the grocery store.

**REUSE:** Means to use an item again. Refill water bottles, wash dishes and containers instead of using disposable, mend or repair the things you have before buying new, and donate clothes and toys to be used by someone else.

**RECYCLE:** Means to make a new thing out of an old one. Recycle cans, bottles and newspapers. Participate in local environmental initiatives like recycling drives.

**REBUY:** Means to purchase items that have already been used or recycled. Shop at thrift and consignment stores and when possible buy items that have been made from recycled materials.

# Summer Fitness Program

Choose an aerobic or strength exercise for each day. Record exercises on the Fitness Log in each section and tally fitness days on the Incentive Contract Calendars. Exercises to choose from are at that back of the book and instruction videos are at **www.SummerFitActivities.com**.

| | Date | Stretch | Activity | Time |
|---|---|---|---|---|
| 1. | *examples:* June 4 | Run in place | Sky Reach | 7 min |
| 2. | June 5 | Toe Touches | Bottle Curls | 15 min |
| 3. | | | | |
| 4. | | | | |
| 5. | | | | |

**Warm Up!** Get ready to exercise by stretching and moving around.

**Stretch!** Move your head slowly side to side, try to touch each shoulder. Now move your head forward, touch your chin to your chest, then look up and as far back as you can. Try to touch your back with the back of your head.

Touch your toes when standing. Bend over at the waist and touch the end of your toes or the floor. Hold this position for 10 seconds.

**Move!** Walk or jog in place for 3-5 minutes to warm up before you exercise. Shake your arms and roll your shoulders when you are finished.

Find out where your child needs a little extra practice!

**1. Write as numbers.**

a. Two million six hundred fifty –four thousand = _____

b. Six million nine hundred forty-three thousand six hundred twelve = _____

**2. Round to the nearest hundred.**

a. 543 = _____     b. 1,489 = _____     c. 6,786 = _____     d. 12,490 = _____

**3. Round to the nearest thousand.**

a. 4,578 = _____     b. 3,209 = _____     c. 12,891 = _____     d. 28,399 = _____

**4. Round to the nearest hundred thousand.**

a. 176,987 = _____          b. 560,821 = _____          c. 601,999 = _____

**5. Write each decimal as a fraction.**

a. .6 = _____     b. .55 = _____     c. .25 = _____     d. 3.8 = _____     e.  1.4 = _____

**6. Add or subtract.**

| a. | 17.05 | b. | 50,000 | c. | 47.60 | d. | 16,794 |
|----|-------|----|--------|----|-------|----|--------|
|    | - 5.13 |   | - 581  |    | - 39.54 |  | - 487  |

**7. Multiply or divide.**

a.     1,429
          x 5

b.     5 | 1600

c.     12,506
          x 22

**8. There are 56 bags of flour on a platform.  Each bag weighs 104 pounds.  How much do all the bags weigh together?** _____

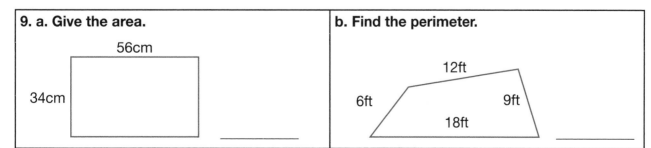

**9. a. Give the area.**

56cm

34cm

_____

**b. Find the perimeter.**

12ft

6ft          9ft

18ft

_____

**10. List the first 10 multiples of 6.** _____

**11. List the factors of 6 and 12. Circle the greatest common factor.**

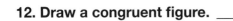
_____

**12. Draw a congruent figure.** _____     _____

| 13. Draw two lines of symmetry through the shape. | 14. Draw a right angle. |
|---|---|
| 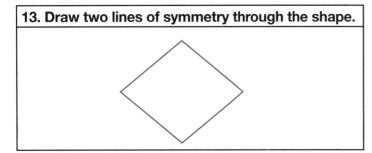 |  |

**15. Label the triangles: equilateral, acute, or right.**

| a. | b. | c. |
|---|---|---|
|  _____ |  _____ | 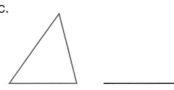 _____ |

**16. Look at the numbers 20, 22, 25, 34, 39.  Find the...**

a. mean = _____     b. median = _____     c. range = _____

**17. Look at the number 7,564,391. Find the...**

| millions place? _____ | hundred-thousands place? _____ | ten-thousands place? _____ |
|---|---|---|
| thousands place? _____ | hundreds place? _____ | ones place? _____ |

**18. Draw a line 3.5 inches.**

**19. Add or subtract the fractions.**

a. 3/5 + 1/5 = _____     b. 9/12 - 3/12 = _____     c. 3/8 + 4/8 = _____     d. 12/15 -8/15 = ____

4-5 • © Summer Fit Activities™

SummerFitActivities.com

**20. Write the contraction for each set of words.**

a. I am = _____          c. you are = _____          e. we will = _____

b. they are = _____     d. it is = _____              f. he is = _____

**21. Write an antonym for each word.**

a. quickly = _____     b. asleep = _____     c. interesting = _____     d. wet = _____

**22. Write a synonym for each word.**

a. smart = _____     b. skinny = _____     c. happy = _____     d. tired = _____

**23. Circle the correct word.**

a. I got a new (pear, pair) of shoes.          b. The cake calls for one cup of (flower, flour).

**24. Use the correct ending punctuation.**

a. How old are you _____     b. Ouch _____ That hurt_____     c. I love to swim _____

**25. Fill in a comma (,) colon (: ) or period (.)**

a. Salt Lake City Utah     b. February 2 1993     c. 4 15 p m     d. I like apples grapes and banana

**26. Circle the verbs.**

The dogs ran and played in the rain.

**27. Circle the adjectives in the sentence.**

My favorite uncle picked me up from baseball practice in his new, red car.

**28. Circle the nouns.**

The tiny mouse scurried quickly into the hole in the wall.

**29. Circle the pronouns in the following passage.**

Sally invited me to her birthday party.  We are going to eat pizza.  It will be so much fun.

**30. Write these words in alphabetical order: really, ran, rain, reject, rowing.**

**31. Write a plural for each singular word.**

a. fish = _____          c. dog=_____          e. duck = _____

b. mouse = _____          d. man=_____          f. fox = _____

**32. Underline the root words.**

a. watered          b.  flowering          c.  rewrite          d.  unbutton

**33. Write the abbreviation for each word.**

a. Avenue = _____          b. doctor = _____          c. inch = _____          d. January = _____

**34. Circle the word divided into syllables correctly.**

a.  dis creet ly          b. disc reet ly          c. di screet ly          d. d is creet ly

**35. Circle the letters that make the "f" sound.**

a. photograph          b. alphabet          c. enough          d. half          e. tough

**36. Fill in the blanks with is, are, was, were.**

a. We _____ going to a movie tomorrow.          c.  My favorite color _____ red.

b. I _____ in 4th grade last year.          d. Where _____ you born?

**37. Use the suffixes ly, est, less, and ful to make a new word.**

a. quick _____          b. quiet _____          c. help _____          d. harm _____

**38. Add capital letters and punctuation to make the sentences correct.**

my name is elizabeth and i was born january 30 1999 in omaha nebraska

**39. Write the past tense for each verb.**

a. swim = _____          b. draw = _____          c. sing = _____          d. drink = _____          e. run = _____

4

4-5 • © Summer Fit Activities™

# INCENTIVE CONTRACT CALENDAR

My parents and I agree that if I complete this section of

and read _____ minutes a day, my reward will be _____

Child Signature: _____    Parent Signature: _____

| Day 1 | | | Day 6 | | |
|---|---|---|---|---|---|
| Day 2 | | | Day 7 | | |
| Day 3 | | | Day 8 | | |
| Day 4 | | | Day 9 | | |
| Day 5 | | | Day 10 | | |

 Color the ✏ for each day of activities completed.

 Color the 📖 for each day of reading completed.

 Fill in how many exercise days completed _____

 Parents initial at end of each completed section _____

# Summer Explorer

## Discover New Things to Play and Do!

- Visit the library and get a card if you do not have one.

- Make a fort out of blankets and sheets.

- Make a biodegradable bird feeder and hang it in the yard.

- Have a lemonade stand get your friends to help.

- Play flashlight tag.

- Visit a fire station. Does your family have a plan of what to do in case of fire? Plan a family fire drill.

- Sign up for a free summer reading program at your local bookstore.

- Go for a walk.

- Look up and find figures in the clouds.

- Play an outdoor game like "Simon Says" or "Kick the Can" with family or friends.

- Go for a bike ride.

- Pick up trash around your neighborhood and recycle.

- Find an ant colony. Drop some crumbs and observe what happens. Stay away from fire ants.

- Build a castle or fort out of Legos or blocks.

- Use a recycled plastic bag to create a parachute that will slowly fall to the ground.

- Watch a sunrise or sunset, paint a picture of it.

- Run through the sprinklers.

- Make S'mores and tell ghost stories under the stars.

- Create an obstacle course. Invite your friends and time them to see how fast they complete it.

## Biodegradable Birdfeeder

1 Collect your supplies: peanut butter, birdseed, oranges, and string for hanging.

2 Tie a long string around the pinecone or toilet roll before spreading peanut butter on them and rolling in birdseed. Cut an orange in half, scoop out fruit and fill with birdseed. Attach strings to hang feeder in branch.

3 Hang your bird treat in the yard and watch for your feathered friends to come and feast.

 **North Star**

**Read the passage then answer the questions below.**

Polaris, otherwise known as the North Star, is one of the most well-known stars. It is called the North Star because it shines directly above the North Pole and can be seen only in the Northern Hemisphere. The North Star never seems to move, and all the other constellations appear to revolve around it. Because of its position in the sky, Polaris has been used for many years as a navigational tool. People look to the North Star to give them direction, and sailors use it to help navigate the oceans.

The Little Dipper

The North Star

The Big Dipper

The easiest way to find Polaris is to find the Big Dipper in the northern part of the sky. The stars that form the outer edge of the Big Dipper's cup are called the pointer stars because they point directly to the North Star. Follow an imaginary line from these two stars, and it will lead you to Polaris, which is the brightest star in the Little Dipper.

| | |
|---|---|
| 1. The North Star is well known because _____. <br><br> A.  It is the biggest star. <br><br> B.  It is always in the same position in the sky. <br><br> C.  It cannot be found easily. <br><br> D.  It is in the South Pole. <br><br><br> 2. The Constellation that points to the North Star is _____. <br><br> A.  Draco   C.  Leo <br><br> B.  Orion   D.  The Big Dipper <br><br><br> 3. Polaris can only be seen in the _____ Hemisphere. <br><br> A.  Southern   C.  Eastern <br><br> B.  Western   D.  Northern | 4. What is the main idea of the story? <br><br> _____ <br><br> _____ <br><br> _____ <br><br> _____ <br><br> _____ <br><br> _____ <br><br> _____ <br><br><br> Underline the topic sentence in each paragraph. |

## Place Value

How many hundreds are there in 6,000?     60 hundreds because 60 x 100 = 6,000

**Write how many tens are in each number.**

1. 500 = _____ tens          4. 800 = _____ tens          7. 2,800 = _____ tens

2. 300 = _____ tens          5. 1,500 = _____ tens        8. 100 = _____ tens

3. 1,000 = _____ tens        6. 2,600 = _____ tens        9. 5,400 = _____ tens

**What is the value of 5 in each of these numbers?**

| | |
|---|---|
| 10. 59 = _____ | 12. 175 = _____ |
| 11. 5,168 = _____ | 13. 59,321 = _____ |

**Answer the following place value questions about the number 5,324,718.**

14. What is the value of the 5?_____

15. What is the value of 1?_____

16. What digit is in the hundred thousands place?_____

17. How many thousands in this number?_____

18. What number is in the ones place?_____

19. What is the value of 2?_____

## Choose your STRENGTH exercise!

**Exercise for today:**

_____

**Day 1**

Recored in Fitness Log

 **Contractions**

A contraction is a shortened form of a word or a group of words with the missing letters marked by an apostrophe.

**Write the words that have been combined to make a contraction.**

1. can't _____

2. wouldn't _____

3. they're _____

4. it's _____

5. haven't _____

6. wasn't _____

7. didn't _____

8. you're _____

9. she's _____

10. he's _____

11. aren't _____

12. won't _____

13. they'll _____

14. don't _____

15. hasn't _____

16. couldn't _____

**Add or subtract.**

1.  302
    - 154
    _____

4.  6,798
    + 3,236
    _____

7.  172
    − 89
    _____

10.  94, 286
     − 46,143
     _____

2.  205
    - 167
    _____

5.  86.54
    + 58.67
    _____

8.  416
    + 248
    _____

11.  79.30
     + 48.78
     _____

3.  8,413
    + 3,450
    _____

6.  187.67
    + 156.89
    _____

9.  5,682
    − 3,447
    _____

12.  245.98
     − 138.79
     _____

**What is the value of 9 in these numbers.**

13. 19 _____

15. 298 _____

17. 976 _____

14. 9,865 _____

16 92,156 _____

18. 967,234 _____

**Write the numbers in expanded form.**

19. 976 = _____

20. 9,865 = _____

21. 92,156 = _____

## Choose your **AEROBIC** exercise!

### Exercise for today:

_____

Recored in
Fitness Log

**Day 2**

## Homophones

**Day 3**

**Homophones are words that sound the same but are spelled differently and have different meanings.**

**Choose the correct homophone from the list to complete each sentence.**

| pair | pear | knew | new | there | their |
|------|------|------|-----|-------|-------|
| to | too | two | through | threw | our | hour |

1. My brother turned _____ years old last Saturday.

2. I ate _____ much candy at the movie.

3. We are going _____ ride our bikes _____ the park.

4. I practice the piano for one _____ every day.

5. We are having a 4th of July party at _____ house.

6. You have to walk _____ the park to get to the duck pond.

7. Hank _____ the winning pitch at the game on Monday.

8. I got a new _____ of shoes for my birthday.

9. My grandma has a _____ tree in her backyard.

10. _____ are 6 people in my family.

11. My cousins brought _____ new puppy to our house.

12. My sister _____ we were throwing her a surprise party.

13. Some _____ neighbors moved into the house next door.

**Write the numbers in standard or word form.**

1. 8,734 _____

2. 502,356 _____

3. 12,567 _____

4. 67,902 _____

5. Five thousand, three hundred sixty two _____

6. Ten thousand, nine hundred seventy-one _____

7. One hundred eight thousand, six hundred fifty-four _____

8. Two million, one hundred fifteen thousand, six hundred twenty one _____

9. What number has 5 ones, 3 hundreds, 6 tens and 8 thousands? _____

10. What number has 15 thousands, 9 tens, 4 hundreds and 8 ones? _____

## Choose your STRENGTH exercise!

**Exercise for today:**

_____

**Day 3**

**Read the passage about birds of prey. Then, answer the questions below.**

Birds of prey are constantly on the lookout for their next meal.  Whether watching for prey from the treetops or soaring through the air, birds of prey are always hunting.  Birds of prey are unique because they hunt other animals and eat their flesh.  These birds use their sharp talons not their beaks to catch their prey.  They have exceptionally good vision and a hooked beak.

The Eagle is one of the largest birds of prey, and is an excellent hunter.  Eagles hunt during the daytime using their powerful legs and feet as their weapons.  Catching its victim by surprise, the eagle will swoop down and use its talons to scoop up the unsuspecting prey.

The owl is another great hunter and is one of the few birds that fly at night.  Unlike other birds, the owl has forward facing eyes so it is able to follow its prey with both eyes.  The owl's silent flight and excellent hearing help make it a very successful hunter.

Vultures are unique to the other birds of prey because they primarily eat dead and decaying animals, therefore they have no need for powerful talons.  Vultures have bald heads to prevent their feathers from getting dirty during feeding.  They are equipped with long, broad wings that are built for soaring.  Their sharp eyes and keen sense of smell allow them to see dead animals from far away.

Birds of prey are interesting to learn about and fascinating to see.

**Fill in the blanks using words from the word bank:**

| excellent | largest | clean | dead | night | prey | talons | eyes | bald |
|---|---|---|---|---|---|---|---|---|

Birds of _____ eat other animals.  They have _____ vision and sharp

_____.  The Eagle is one of the _____ birds of prey.  Owls have forward

facing _____ and hunt at _____.  Vultures have _____ heads to

keep their feathers _____ while feasting on _____ animals.

**Underline the topic sentence of each paragraph.**

**Round each number to the nearest hundred.**    Example: 167 = 200

| | | |
|---|---|---|
| 1. 358 _____ | 4. 439 _____ | 7. 298 _____ |
| 2. 674 _____ | 5. 329 _____ | 8. 150 _____ |
| 3. 814 _____ | 6. 785 _____ | 9. 182 _____ |

**Round each number to the nearest thousand.**  Example: 5, 210 = 5,000

| | | |
|---|---|---|
| 10. 4,897 _____ | 13. 6,478 _____ | 16. 7,934 _____ |
| 11. 2,367 _____ | 14. 3,820 _____ | 17. 5,567 _____ |
| 12. 1,308 _____ | 15. 2,600 _____ | 18.1,709 _____ |

**Round each number to the nearest ten thousand.**

19. 56,378 = _____     21. 78,946 = _____

20. 124, 567 = _____     22. 469,543 = _____

## Choose your AEROBIC exercise!

### Exercise for today:

_____

**Day 4**

Recored in
Fitness Log

# HONESTY

Value

*Honesty means being fair, truthful, and trustworthy. Honesty includes telling the truth and being fair even when it is not popular and may be difficult.*

**Abraham Lincoln** was born in a log cabin on February 12, 1809. Lincoln's mother died when he was only nine years old, so he had to work hard to help his father on the farm. Lincoln was not able to attend school very often, but he loved to read and do math. He read many books and learned on his own. As a young man, Lincoln worked on a farm, as a postmaster, and then as the shopkeeper of his own store. He was honest in all his businesses and people trusted him.

Lincoln became a lawyer and was a senator and congressman before he was elected president of the United States of America. Lincoln was president during the United States of America's bloody Civil War and was under constant pressure by many different groups who wanted him to support their own ideas. Lincoln displayed strength, courage, and honesty by doing what was best for the United States of America and the people that he swore to lead.

**Unscramble the letters to make words from the story above.**

**1.** vaslrye _____

**3.** perdsiten _____

**2.** noHste bAe _____

**4.** strudte _____

**5.** Research the USA's Civil War on the internet or at a library. Write down an example of how Lincoln's honesty affected the outcome of the war.

_____

_____

_____

_____

# Value: HONESTY

Being honest means to be truthful in what you say and do. It means that you do not lie, cheat or steal. Sometimes this can be difficult, especially when we are scared or ashamed about something we did. Sometimes it takes courage to be honest, especially when it is uncomfortable.

"Whatever you are,
be a good one"
-Abe Lincoln

**What does honesty look like? Choose an honest action below and draw a picture to represent it in the picture frame.**

- I cheat on a test.
- I keep a promise.
- I play fair.
- I take a candy bar from the store without paying.
- I take money out of my dad's wallet without asking.
- I find $5.00 at the library and take it to the front desk.

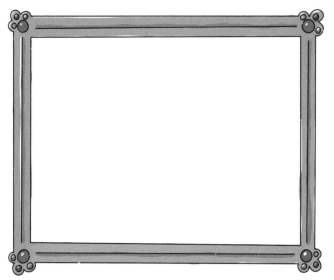

## HONESTY PLEDGE

I promise to tell the truth every day. I will be honest in what I do and what I say.

_____

My Signature

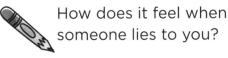
How does it feel when someone lies to you?

_____

_____

_____

_____

**Day 5**

**Choose a Play or Exercise Activity!**

4-5 • © Summer Fit Activities™

# Summer Fitness Log

Choose your exercise activity each day from the Aerobic and Strength Activities in the back of the book. Record the date, stretch, activity and how long you performed your exercise activity below. Fill in how many days you complete your fitness activity on your Incentive Contract Calendars.

| | Date | Stretch | Activity | Time |
|---|---|---|---|---|
| examples: | June 4 | Run in place | Sky Reach | 7 min |
| | June 5 | Toe Touches | Bottle Curls | 15 min |
| 1. | | | | |
| 2. | | | | |
| 3. | | | | |
| 4. | | | | |
| 5. | | | | |
| 6. | | | | |
| 7. | | | | |
| 8. | | | | |
| 9. | | | | |
| 10. | | | | |

I promise to do my best for me. I exercise to be healthy and active. I am awesome because I am me.

Child Signature: _____

# Summer Journal I

Write about your favorite outdoor summer activity.

Example: Camping, swimming or biking.

4-5 • © Summer Fit Activities™

## Abbreviations

**Read each sentence write the abbreviation for the underlined words.**

**Ex. A foot is 12 <u>inches</u> long. <u>in.</u>**

1. My grandmother lives on Maple <u>Avenue.</u> _____

2. <u>Doctor</u> Smith gave me a complete checkup. _____

3. I am excited to meet my new teacher <u>Mister</u> William. _____

4. The library is on Pine <u>Street.</u> _____

5. The recipe called for 1 <u>teaspoon</u> of baking soda. _____

6. A <u>pound</u> of apples cost $1.25. _____

**7. Draw a line from each word to its abbreviation.**

| | |
|---|---|
| oz. | dozen |
| cm. | yard |
| doz. | quart |
| ft. | ounce |
| qt. | week |
| yd. | feet |
| wk. | centimeter |

# Fractions

A fraction is a way of representing the division of a "whole" into "parts." Reduce each fraction to its lowest terms.

**Example.** $\dfrac{5}{10} = \dfrac{1}{2}$

1. $\dfrac{3}{6} =$          4. $\dfrac{6}{12} =$          7. $\dfrac{7}{21} =$

2. $\dfrac{9}{15} =$          5. $\dfrac{4}{8} =$          8. $\dfrac{10}{30} =$

3. $\dfrac{3}{18} =$          6. $\dfrac{2}{8} =$          9. $\dfrac{4}{16} =$

---

**Write an equivalent fraction for each fraction.**

10. Ex. 1/2 = 2/4          11. 5/15 = _____          12. 1/4 = _____

---

**Convert these fractions to decimals:**

13. 6/10 = _____          16. 5/10 = _____          19. 8/10 = _____

14. 5/100 = _____          17. 4/100 = _____          20. 7/100 = _____

15. 3/100 = _____          18. 1/100 = _____          21. 3/10 = _____

## Choose your AEROBIC exercise!

**Exercise for today:**

Recored in Fitness Log

**Day 6**

## Word Families

Word families are sets of words that have commonality.

Inside each birdhouse is a word family with one word that doesn't belong. Cross out the word that doesn't belong and think of a name for each group of words.

1.

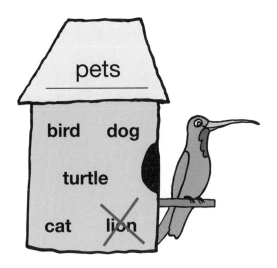

pets
_____

bird    dog

turtle

cat    ~~lion~~

2.

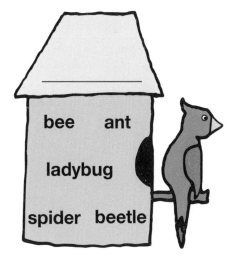

_____

bee    ant

ladybug

spider   beetle

3.

_____

apple    grape

strawberry

orange  carrot

4.

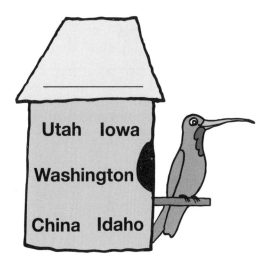

_____

Utah   Iowa

Washington

China   Idaho

5.

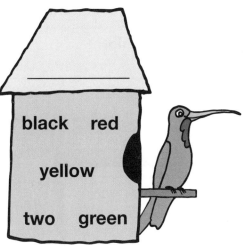

_____

black    red

yellow

two    green

6.

_____

sour    sugar

bitter

spicy   sweet

## Mixed Practice

**Solve.**

| | | | | | |
|---|---|---|---|---|---|
| 1. | 564<br>+ 248 | 5. | 628<br>+ 436 | 9. | 289<br>+ 465 |
| 2. | 462<br>+ 235 | 6. | 3,560<br>+ 2,525 | 10. | 3,136<br>+ 1,240 |
| 3. | 3,560<br>+ 2,486 | 7. | 23,456<br>+ 14,489 | 11. | 36,823<br>+ 28,345 |
| 4. | 7,840<br>+ 2,657 | 8. | 34,235<br>+ 20,421 | 12. | 234,022<br>+ 102,957 |

**13. Circle the odd numbers and underline the even numbers.**

| | | | | | |
|---|---|---|---|---|---|
| 12 | 17 | 21 | 16 | 48 | 50 |
| 111 | 124 | 148 | 267 | 290 | 508 |
| 146 | 340 | 521 | 470 | 1,268 | 1,987 |

## Choose your STRENGTH exercise!

**Exercise for today:**

**Day 7**

Recored in
Fitness Log

4-5 • © Summer Fit Activities™

## Idioms

**"Oops, I let the cat out of the bag."**

Idioms are phrases or expressions that can't be figured out by looking up the meaning of each individual word. For example, "letting the cat out of the bag," has nothing to do with a cat; rather, it means to reveal a secret.

**Circle the correct meaning of each idiom.**

1. As the team's newest member, he was the "low man on the totem pole."

| Shortest one on the team | Least important person on the team. |

2. I walked in the door and "right off the bat" Mom asked me to clean my room.

| Right away. | Put my bat away after practice. |

3. It was "raining cats and dogs" so the picnic was cancelled.

| Cats and dogs were falling out of the trees. | Raining heavily |

4. I've been saving all summer for a bike, but it's still "just a drop in the bucket."

| A drop of water falling into a bucket. | A small amount of money. |

5. I'm "down to the wire" on my book report; it's due tomorrow.

| Running out of time. | Writing a report on wire. |

6. When you feel like talking back to your parents, "bite your tongue."

| Don't talk back no matter what. | Bite your tongue when talking with your parents. |

**Write a sentence using these idioms.**

7. "feeling blue " _____

_____

_____

8. "eyes at the back of her head" _____

_____

_____

9. "going bananas" _____

_____

_____

# Money Matters

Using the least number of bills and coins, write how many of each is needed to equal the total given.

| | $5 | $1 | quarter | dime | nickel | penny |
|---|---|---|---|---|---|---|
| 1. $5.67 | 1 | | 2 | 1 | 1 | 2 |
| 2. $3.28 | | | | | | |
| 3. $7.56 | | | | | | |
| 4. $9.89 | | | | | | |
| 5. $10.72 | | | | | | |
| 6. $4.75 | | | | | | |
| 7. $6.49 | | | | | | |

8. How much money is shown?  $ _____

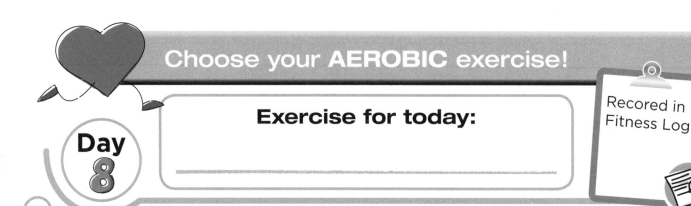

Choose your **AEROBIC** exercise!

**Exercise for today:**

Recored in Fitness Log

**Day 8**

4-5 • © Summer Fit Activities™

SummerFitActivities.com

## The Brain

**Read the passage below and answer the questions.**

Your brain is like a computer that keeps your body working around the clock, day and night. Your brain looks like a large walnut and is protected inside your skull. Nerves inside your brain send messages to your body almost instantaneously. There are three major parts of your brain, and each part has its own special job to keep things running smoothly.

The main part of your brain, called the cerebrum, has two halves called hemispheres. The left hemisphere controls the right side of your body, and the right hemisphere controls the left. The cerebrum controls all of your body movements, like running, walking, jumping, throwing a ball, or holding a pencil. It also controls your five senses, as well as your thoughts and speech.

The part of your brain below the cerebrum is the cerebellum. The cerebellum is an important but smaller part of the brain located at the base of the skull. It looks like a mini version of the cerebrum and in fact, cerebellum means "little brain" in Latin. The cerebellum controls your balance by making sure all your muscles work together. It controls voluntary movements, basic memory, and also receives and processes information from your eyes and ears.

The third and smallest part of your brain is the brain stem and connects to your spinal cord. All information that comes from the brain travels through the brain stem to the rest of the body. The brain stem is responsible for voluntary and involuntary movement such as breathing, sleeping, digesting food, and the beating of your heart.

**Fill in the blanks.**

1. There are _____ main parts of the brain.

2. The _____ inside your brain send _____ to your body.

3. The largest part of the brain is the _____.

4. The cerebrum controls your body movements, the five _____,

    your thinking, and _____.

5. The _____ means "little brain" in Latin.

6. The smallest part of the brain is the _____ _____.

7. It connects to the _____ _____.

8. **Circle all the plural words in the passage above.**

**Solve.**

| | | | |
|---|---|---|---|
| 1.  539 x 3 | 5.  673 x 8 | 9.  296 x 5 | 13.  897 x 4 |
| 2.  2,389 x 5 | 6.  4,590 x 4 | 10.  6,239 x 9 | 14.  8,875 x 2 |
| 3.  9,367 x 8 | 7.  7,127 x 7 | 11.  9,020 x 3 | 15.  5,875 x 2 |
| 4.  1,938 x 9 | 8.  3,348 x 5 | 12.  9,876 x 6 | 16.  6,549 x 4 |

**17. Finish the pattern:**

12, 24, 36, _____, _____, _____, _____, _____, _____, _____, _____, _____

## Choose your STRENGTH exercise!

**Exercise for today:**

Recored in Fitness Log

**Day 9**

# COMPASSION

**Compassion is caring about the feelings and needs of others and includes helping those in need.**

Value

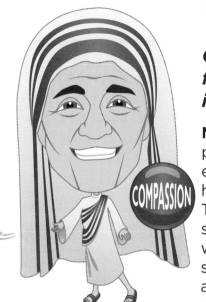

**Mother Teresa** was one of the most compassionate people the world has ever known. She devoted her entire life to serving others and spreading love and hope to those in need. As a young woman, Mother Teresa chose to serve as a missionary. She served selflessly, caring for people in India and around the world who had nobody to care for them: the poor, sick, dying, and alone. Her compassion was endless, and she treated every person she met with love, dignity, and respect.

Mother Teresa saw the beauty in everyone and turned her back on no one. She and the Missionaries of Charity opened orphanages for abandoned children and homes for the sick and dying. She collected people off the streets of Calcutta, India, and took them in to care for them. Mother Teresa won many awards for her work, including the Nobel Peace Prize. She told people that "love begins at home and it is not how much we do that matters, rather it is how much love we put into the things we do." Even when she herself was in poor health, she continued to help others. Mother Teresa showed enormous amounts of compassion, and her acts of generosity, kindness, and love are an inspiration to all.

**1.** Name four groups of people Mother Teresa helped.

_____     _____

_____     _____

**2.** What were three of Mother Teresa's most compassionate qualities?

_____     _____

_____

**3.** In what country is the city of Calcutta located?

_____

**4.** Look up India on a map or globe. Find Calcutta.

# Value: COMPASSION

Having compassion means showing kindness, caring and a willingness to help others who may be sick, hurt, poor, or in need. When you have compassion you are putting yourself in someone else's shoes and really feeling for them. You can do this in very small ways for example when your friend trips and falls. You can do this in larger ways when someone you know does not have enough food to eat.

"Love and compassion are necessities not luxuries. Without them, humanity cannot survive."
– Dalai Lama

**Unscramble the letters to reveal the traits of being a Hero of Compassion.**

dnik                    ielgnsnti

ufltuhgtoh              rstceandoei

aricgn                  ronfmoicgt

udantnesinrgd           avber

epilngh                 tpaenti

Make a "Compassion Jar". Cut out several slips of paper and write on each a way to show compassion. For example: Hold the door for someone, smile at a stranger, or read to a younger child. Choose one to do each day.

(kind) (thoughtful) (caring) (understanding) (helping)
(listening) (considerate) (comforting) (brave) (patient)

# INCENTIVE CONTRACT CALENDAR

My parents and I agree that if I complete this section of

## Summer Fit Activities™

and read _____ minutes a day, my reward will be _____

Child Signature: _____     Parent Signature: _____

| | | | | | |
|---|---|---|---|---|---|
| Day 1 | ✏️ | 📖 | Day 6 | ✏️ | 📖 |
| Day 2 | ✏️ | 📖 | Day 7 | ✏️ | 📖 |
| Day 3 | ✏️ | 📖 | Day 8 | ✏️ | 📖 |
| Day 4 | ✏️ | 📖 | Day 9 | ✏️ | 📖 |
| Day 5 | ✏️ | 📖 | Day 10 | ✏️ | 📖 |

Color the  for each day of activities completed.

Color the  for each day of reading completed.

 Fill in how many exercise days completed _____

 Parents initial at end of each completed section _____

# Summer Explorer

## Discover New Things to Play and Do!

- Play in the rain. Make mud pies and jump in puddles.

- Have a book exchange with your friends.

- Finger paint.

- Make your own musical instruments out of cardboard boxes and perform a song.

- Create a healthy dinner menu for your family.

- Visit a lake, river, or pond. Bring a notebook to do some nature drawings.

- Make your own bubble solution. Go outside and make some enormous bubbles.

- Pick wildflowers and arrange them in a glass or jar.

- Draw a flipbook.

- Make cookies for a neighbor — deliver them with a parent.

- Go to the park with a friend.

- Sign up for a free project at Home Depot, Lowes, or Michaels.

- Make a scavenger hunt to do with friends or family.

- Plant something: flowers, vegetables, herbs, a tree.

- Read to a younger sibling.

- Make a photo album or scrapbook.

- Try a new cookie recipe.

- Have a water balloon fight.

- Help an elderly neighbor weed his/her garden.

- Paint or draw a self-portrait.

## Giant Bubbles

6 cups Water
1/2 cup Dish Soap (Dawn blue)
1/2 cup Cornstarch
1 TBSP Baking Powder
1 TBSP Glycerin
(Glycerin found in cake decoration aisle at craft store)

1 Slowly mix together in large bucket or dishpan.

2 Let solution sit for 1-2 hours.

3 Tie a length of string between two straws to make a bubble wand or use store bought wands. The bigger your wand, the bigger your bubbles!

4-5 • © Summer Fit Activities™

## A or An, This or These

**Choose "a" or "an" to complete each sentence.**

1. We saw _____ enormous elephant at the zoo.

2. I am on _____ little league baseball team.

3. My favorite sea creature is _____ electric eel.

4. I saw _____ snake slither behind the rock.

5. Mom made me _____ egg for breakfast.

6. We have _____ apple tree in the front yard.

7. I got _____ skateboard for my birthday.

8. It is good to carry _____ umbrella on rainy days.

9. My family went on _____ picnic to celebrate Mother's Day.

10. There is _____ anthill on the sidewalk in front of our house.

**Choose "this" or "these" to complete each sentence.**

11. _____ ice cream cone is delicious!

12. Please put _____ books on the table.

13. My birthday is _____ coming Friday.

14. I could look at _____ stars forever!

15. I will be visiting my grandparents at the end of _____ month.

16. "Please wash _____ dishes," my mother asked.

17. The flowers are beautiful _____ summer.

18. My dad says it is good to find hard workers _____ days.

19. I will pick up _____ toys, if you pick up those.

4–5 • © Summer Fit Activities™

# Perimeter and Area

The perimeter is the total distance around a shape. Give the perimeter of each shape.

| | | |
|---|---|---|
| **7 cm**<br><br>**4 cm** | **24 in**<br><br>**12 in** | **35 m**<br><br>**35 m** |
| perimeter = _____ cm | perimeter = _____ in | perimeter = _____ m |

Area is measured in square units. You find the area of a rectangle or square by multiplying the length by the width. Calculate the area of each shape.

| | | |
|---|---|---|
| **4 cm**<br><br>**2 cm** | **3 in**<br><br>**3 in** | **5 ft**<br><br>**3 ft** |
| **Ex.** area = __8__ cm$^2$ | area = _____ in$^2$ | area = _____ ft$^2$ |

## Choose your STRENGTH exercise!

**Exercise for today:**

_____

Recored in
Fitness Log

**Day**
**1**

4-5 • © Summer Fit Activities™

 **Verbs**

**Day 2**

A verb is a word that shows action. A verb tells what a person or thing is doing. Circle the verbs in the following sentences.

1. Susan sings in the church choir.

2. The dog barked all night long.

3. My mom baked me a cake for my birthday.

4. The wind blew over the tree in the front yard.

5. The forward dribbled the ball down the field and scored a goal.

6. Jon David played the guitar in the talent show.

7. I read the book I checked out at the library.

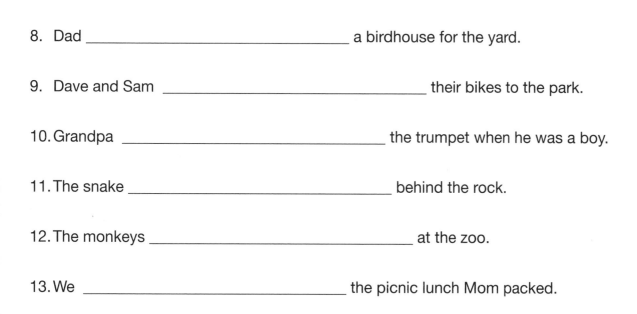

**Write a verb to complete each sentence.**

8. Dad _____ a birdhouse for the yard.

9. Dave and Sam _____ their bikes to the park.

10. Grandpa _____ the trumpet when he was a boy.

11. The snake _____ behind the rock.

12. The monkeys _____ at the zoo.

13. We _____ the picnic lunch Mom packed.

4-5 • © Summer Fit Activities™

**Favorite Pet?**

**Mr. John's 5th grade class took a poll to see what pets the students had. Use the pie graph to answer the questions.**

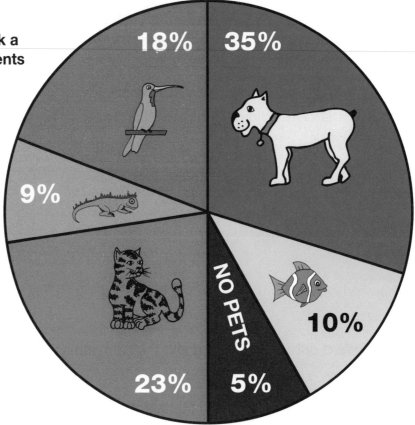

1. What percentage of the students have a dog? _____

2. How many different pets are represented? _____

   Name them: _____

3. What pet has the smallest percentage? _____

4. What percentage of the class has a fish? _____

5. What is the most popular pet? _____

6. What percentage of the students have birds and fish? _____

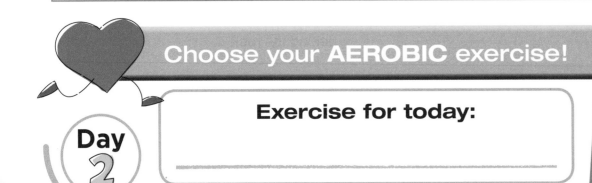

## Choose your AEROBIC exercise!

**Exercise for today:**

_____

**Day 2**

Recored in Fitness Log

## Singular to Plural

**There are many ways to make nouns plural:**

1. Add "s" to most nouns (sock = socks).
2. Nouns that end in s, sh, ch, or x add "es" (bush = bushes).
3. If a noun ends in a consonant and a "y", change "y" to an "i" and add es (puppy = puppies).
4. Some nouns ending in "f" add "s" (handkerchief = handkerchiefs).
5. For some nouns ending in "f" change "f" to a "v" and add "es" (knife = knives).
6. Some nouns stay the same in its plural form (moose = moose).
7. Some nouns have an irregular plural form (woman = women).
8. For words that end in "o" add "s" or "es" (hero = heroes).

**Change each singular noun to a plural using the information above.**

1. lion _____

2. peach _____

3. wolf _____

4. penny _____

5. leaf _____

6. cake _____

7. foot _____

8. mouse _____

9. belief _____

10. girl _____

11. scarf _____

12. baby _____

13. thief _____

14. deer _____

15. man _____

16. bench _____

17. dog _____

18. class _____

19. cat _____

20. toe _____

21. boy _____

22. noun _____

## Compare

Write the correct sign: <, >, or = to solve each problem.

| | | |
|---|---|---|
| 1. 6,785 _____ 6,857 | 6. 6 x 8 _____ 8 x 8 | 11. 3.75 _____ 3.1 |
| 2. 3 x 8,654 _____ 8,654 x 3 | 7. 10 x 10 _____ 200 – 100 | 12. 59 x 100 _____ 590 x 10 |
| 3. 123,320 _____ 133,420 | 8. 5 x 100 _____ 250 – 150 | 13. 100 ÷ 100 _____ 4 ÷ 2 |
| 4. 10 x 9 _____ 100 - 10 | 9. 1/2 _____ 2/4 | 14. 9,037 _____ 9,307 |
| 5. (6 x 3) + 8 _____ 9 + (5 x 6) | 10. 1/3 + 1/3 _____ 1/2 + 1/2 | 15. 7 x 7 _____ 6 x 8 |

**Multiply the decimals.**

16.
   75.6
   x 8
_____

17.
   56.9
   x 3
_____

18.
   95.8
   x 4
_____

19.
   73.4
   x 9
_____

## Choose your STRENGTH exercise!

Recored in
Fitness Log

**Exercise for today:**

_____

**Day 3**

4–5 • © Summer Fit Activities™

## Choose the Correct Word

**Circle the correct word to complete the sentence.**

1. When is (you're, your) birthday?

2. (Their, There, They're) dog had puppies on Saturday.

3. (It's, Its) going to rain today.

4. I am going to (meat, meet) my friends at the movie.

5. My dog hurt his leg but (heel, he'll)  be better soon.

6. (Our, Hour) neighbors are going camping. (They're, Their) leaving on Friday.

7. (Whose, Who's) going to drive us to the park?

8. (You're, Your) going to be late for school!

9. The bird built (it's, its) nest in the apple tree.

10. I got a (knew, new) soccer ball for my birthday.

11. (I'll, Aisle) pick up the cans that rolled into the (I'll, aisle).

12. Do you know (where, wear) Yellowstone National Park is?

13. The pitcher (through, threw) a great game on Saturday.

14.  The (bear, bare) growled to protect her cubs.

15. The sick calf was too (week, weak) to lift (its, it's) head.

The point (0,0) is called the origin. The first coordinate of a plotted point is called the "x" coordinate and moves horizontally from the origin. The second coordinate is called the "y" coordinate and moves vertically from the origin. Plot each pair moving horizontally, then vertically. The first one has been done for you.

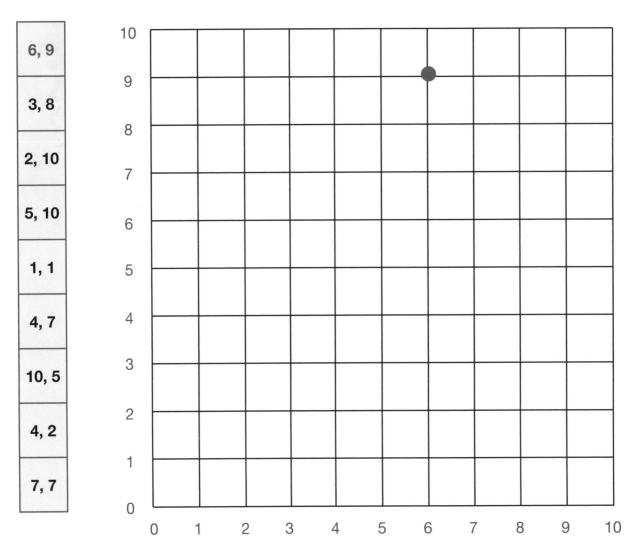

**Name 4 sets of coordinates to form a Square.**

_____  _____  _____  _____

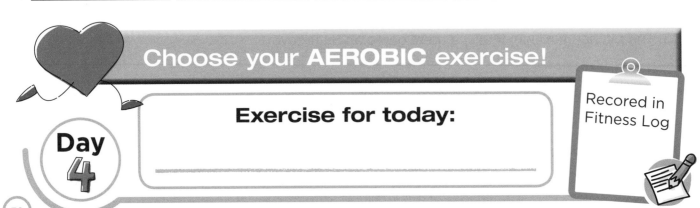

# TRUSTWORTHINESS

*Trustworthiness is being worthy of trust. Being trustworthy means people can count on you and you keep your word.*

Value

**Harriet Tubman** was a slave around the time of the Civil War. Being a slave meant that she had no property, no rights, and had to do whatever her master told her. From a very young age, Harriet had to work hard for no pay, but even as a young girl she dreamed of being free. Although she was small, Harriet was strong and even more strong willed. When she was an adult, Harriet escaped to the North where she finally found freedom; but being free was not enough for Harriet. Harriet knew slavery was wrong and wanted others to be free as well.

Harriet led hundreds of slaves to freedom through the Underground Railroad which was a secret system of hiding places and transportation to help slaves escape. People called abolitionists wanted slavery to end, and there were many people who helped the slaves on their journey to freedom. Harriet made 19 trips to escort slaves to freedom, and each time she risked her life. At one point there was a $40,000 reward offered by slave-owners for her capture. Harriet Tubman represents trustworthiness because people trusted her with their lives, and she never let them down.

**1.** Look up in a dictionary or on the internet the meaning of these words:

freedom: _____

trustworthiness: _____

slavery: _____

abolitionists: _____

strong-willed: _____

reward: _____

**2.** Write a paragraph as if you were a slave who wanted to escape slavery. Include how you felt about slavery, Harriet Tubman, and the Underground Railroad.

_____

_____

_____

_____

# Value: TRUSTWORTHINESS

## FAMILY ACTIVITIES

**Choose one or more activities to do with your family or friends.**

### Let's talk about it...

Talk with your child about keeping a promise. Help them to understand that it is important to think before they promise something. Be consistent when you are making promises to your children either in rewards or punishments. Lead by example and make sure to follow through with what you say.

 Talk about ways you show you are trustworthy. Remember that when you are dishonest and not truthful, people will not trust you. Think about the times you have been trustworthy. Write down at least 5 words that describe how you felt being trusted.

 Talk about what it means to be a trustworthy friend. Make a Friendship bracelet and give it to one of your friends. Let them know they can count on you to be a good friend.

 Write down the word TRUSTWORTHY. How many little words can you make from the letters?

### VALUES ARE A FAMILY AFFAIR

Read more about
**TRUSTWORTHINESS**

**The Trial of Anna Cotman**
By Vivien Alcock

**Summer of My German Soldier**
By Bette Greene

**A Question of Trust**
By Margaret Dane Bawer

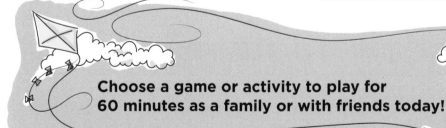

**Choose a game or activity to play for 60 minutes as a family or with friends today!**

## Day 5

### Choose a Play or Exercise Activity!

# Summer Fitness Log

Choose your exercise activity each day from the Aerobic and Strength Activities in the back of the book. Record the date, stretch, activity and how long you performed your exercise activity below. Fill in how many days you complete your fitness activity on your Incentive Contract Calendars.

| | Date | Stretch | Activity | Time |
|---|---|---|---|---|
| examples: | June 4 | Run in place | Sky Reach | 7 min |
| | June 5 | Toe Touches | Bottle Curls | 15 min |
| 1. | | | | |
| 2. | | | | |
| 3. | | | | |
| 4. | | | | |
| 5. | | | | |
| 6. | | | | |
| 7. | | | | |
| 8. | | | | |
| 9. | | | | |
| 10. | | | | |

I promise to do my best for me. I exercise to be healthy and active. I am awesome because I am me.

Child Signature: _____

4-5 • © Summer Fit Activities™

# Summer Journal II

Write about your family vacation.

4-5 • © Summer Fit Activities™

## Sentences

A **declarative** sentence is a sentence made in the form of a statement. An **interrogative** sentence asks a question. An **imperative** sentence gives a command. An **exclamatory** sentence shows strong feeling.

**Write the correct punctuation after each sentence and label the sentence: declarative, interrogative, imperative, or exclamatory.**

1. Pass the salt _____     _____

2. Are you going swimming today _____     _____

3. My dad took me to the Air and Space Museum _____     _____

4. I won first place in the contest _____     _____

5. Please shut the door _____     _____

6. What a mess _____     _____

7. How old are you _____     _____

8. Look out _____ A snake _____     _____

**9. Write an example of each kind of sentence: declarative, interrogative, imperative, and exclamatory.**

Declarative: _____

Interrogative: _____

Imperative:_____

Exclamatory: _____

Day 6


4-5 • © Summer Fit Activities

SummerFitActivities.com

## Adding Decimals

Add decimal equations to solve each problem.

| | | |
|---|---|---|
| **1.**  52.46  + 43.50 | **6.**  67.90  + 34.26 | **11.**  78.65  + 23.57 |
| **2.**  88.23  + 72.83 | **7.**  41.13  + 38.07 | **12.**  52.89  + 34.19 |
| **3.**  24.56  + 18.45 | **8.**  84.93  + 27.68 | **13.**  34.56  + 29.14 |
| **4.**  182.20  + 134.15 | **9.**  245.98  + 199.12 | |
| **5.**  146.75  + 109.23 | **10.**  895.32  + 602.41 |  |

## Choose your **AEROBIC** exercise!

**Exercise for today:**

Recored in Fitness Log

**Day 6**

4-5 • © Summer Fit Activities™

**Big bike**

**Bigger bike**

Comparative adjectives compare two things by adding "er" or using the word "more."

Superlative adjectives compare three or more things by adding "est" or "most."

**Add er, est, more, or most to the adjective in parenthesis.**

1. My bike is _____ than my brother's bike.  (new)

2. Dogs are _____ than cats. (noisy)

3. Apples are the _____ fruit. (delicious)

4. A cheetah is _____ than a lion.  (fast)

5. The _____ book I ever read was about a mouse and a motorcycle. (funny)

6. Turtles are the _____ of all the reptiles. (fascinating)

7. I am the _____ runner in my class.  (slow)

8. Purple grapes are _____ than green grapes. (sweet)

9. The piano piece I am learning is the _____ piece I have ever

   played. (difficult)

10. This summer is the _____ summer I can remember. (warm)

## Converting Measurements

Convert the measurements using the measurement index.

| | |
|---|---|
| 12 inches = 1 foot | 5, 280 feet = 1 mile |
| 3 feet = 1 yard | 1,760 yards = 1 mile |

1. 24 inches = _____ feet

2. 48 inches = _____ feet

3. 9 feet = _____ yards

4. 5 yards = _____ feet

5. 18 feet = _____ yards

6. 3,520 yards = _____ miles

7. 72 inches = _____ feet

8. 12 feet = _____ yards

9. 36 feet = _____ yards

10. 3 yards = _____ feet

11. 31,680 feet = _____ miles

12. 24 feet = _____ yards

**Write these numbers from least to greatest.**

13.

| 52,956 | 529 | 52 | 15,295 | 515,295 | 5,295 |
|---|---|---|---|---|---|
| _____ | _____ | _____ | _____ | _____ | _____ |

14.

| 268 | 2,687 | 186 | 268,187 | 28,675 | 27,867 |
|---|---|---|---|---|---|
| _____ | _____ | _____ | _____ | _____ | _____ |

## Choose your STRENGTH exercise!

**Exercise for today:**

_____

Recored in
Fitness Log

**Day 7**

4–5 • © Summer Fit Activities™

A compound word is made when two words are joined to form a new word.
Write the two words that make up each compound word.

Ex. _____ bull _____ + _____ frog _____ = _____ bullfrog _____

1. headache = _____ + _____

_____ _____

2. everywhere = _____ + _____

_____ _____

3. lifeguard = _____ + _____

_____ _____

4. secondhand = _____ + _____

_____ _____

5. homeless = _____ + _____

_____ _____

6. birthday = _____ + _____

_____ _____

7. snakeskin = _____ + _____

_____ _____

8. basketball = _____ + _____

_____ _____

**Solve the story problems.**

1. The bakery ordered 180 pounds of sugar, 150 pounds of flour, and 500 pounds of butter. What is the total weight of the order? _____

2. Sam is saving up for a new bike.  He has $38.76 in his piggy bank. He got $46.00 for his birthday.  If the new bike costs $120.00, how much more does he need to earn?

_____

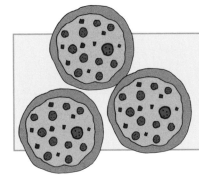

3. Mary's family ordered 3 pizzas.  Each pizza has 10 slices. If Mary's family has 6 people at dinner, how many slices will they get each?

_____

4. The temperatures for the week were: 80°, 82°, 80°, 83°, 75°, 74°, 79°.

What was the average temperature? _____

5. Sam works at the library from 8:00 am until 5:00 pm Monday through Saturday.  He gets a break every day from 12:00 to 1:00.  How many hours does Sam work in a week?

_____

6. It takes 18 hours for one person to build a fence.  If there are three people building the fence, how many hours will it take?

_____

## Choose your AEROBIC exercise!

### Exercise for today:

Recored in Fitness Log

**Day 8**

 **Present and Past Tense**

**Change each present tense word to the past tense.**

| Present: | Past: |
|---|---|
| 1. choose | chose |
| 2. write | |
| 3. throw | |
| 4. run | |
| 5. know | |
| 6. make | |
| 7. ride | |
| 8. grow | |
| 9. sing | |
| 10. feel | |
| 11. sleep | |
| 12. hide | |
| 13. sell | |
| 14. hear | |

**Write a short sentence for each of these words using their past tense.**

15. sleep _____

_____.

16. make _____

_____.

17. choose _____

_____.

18. ride _____

_____.

**Work quickly.**

1. 20 ÷ 4 = _____

2. 16 ÷ 8 = _____

3. 49 ÷ 7 = _____

4. 28 ÷ 4 = _____

5. 35 ÷ 5 = _____

6. 27 ÷ 9 = _____

7. 42 ÷ 7 = _____

8. 90 ÷ 10 = _____

9. 18 ÷ 3 = _____

10. 48 ÷ 6 = _____

11. 54 ÷ 6 = _____

12. 56 ÷ 7 = _____

13. 30 ÷ 3 = _____

14. 24 ÷ 6 = _____

15. 32 ÷ 4 = _____

16. 63 ÷ 7 = _____

**Divide.  If there is a remainder, make sure it is less than the divisor.**

17. 5 ⟌ 393

18. 2 ⟌ 982

19. 4 ⟌ 576

20. 3 ⟌ 2,571

21. 9 ⟌ 3,204

22. 8 ⟌ 5,376

23. 3 ⟌ 2,226

24. 9 ⟌ 8,289

## Choose your STRENGTH exercise!

**Exercise for today:**

_____

Recored in
Fitness Log

**Day**
**9**

4-5 • © Summer Fit Activities™

# SELF-DISCIPLINE

Value

*Self-discipline is to have control of your actions and focus on your goals. Self-discipline includes having self-control, dedication, and commitment to the people and things that are important to you.*

**Stephanie Lopez Cox** knows that she has to work hard to reach her goals. Through self-discipline and dedication she played on the U.S. National Women's Soccer Team and helped lead her team to win the gold medal at the 2008 Beijing Olympics. Although Stephanie is known for her excellent soccer skills, she also lettered in basketball all three years of high school and kept very good grades. Stephanie displays self-discipline through self-control, dedication, and commitment to herself, her goals, and the causes that are important to her. Stephanie grew up in a home that fostered children; she uses the same focus and commitment that made her into a premier athlete, to help others by raising awareness for foster homes. Stephanie is dedicated to bettering the world around her.

**List three things from the story that Stephanie accomplished from being self-disciplined.**

1. _____

2. _____

3. _____

**Think of three things you can accomplish through self-discipline.**

4. _____

5. _____

6. _____

# Value: SELF-DISCIPLINE

## FAMILY ACTIVITIES

**Choose one or more activities to do with your family or friends.**

### Let's talk about it...

Encourage your child to be determined and focused when completing a task or project. Identify a project or sport that your child has not done such as swimming, playing basketball, or tennis. Introduce him/her to it and encourage them to stay involved for a certain amount of time.

Plan to exercise together as a family this week. Have a family walk after dinner. Choose an activity to do together. Hike, bike, swim, dance and play together. At night, play a game of "flashlight tag." Whoever gets "tagged" by the light is "it."

Give up TV for a day, a week, or longer. Instead, spend time outside, reading, or with family and friends.

Plan a sequence of events or activities to do in one day. Before you move on to the next one you must finish the one before it.

## VALUES ARE A FAMILY AFFAIR

Read more about
### SELF-DISCIPLINE

**A Likely Place**
By Paula Fox

**My Side of the Mountain**
By Jean Craighead George

**Island of the Blue Dolphins**
By Scott O'Dell

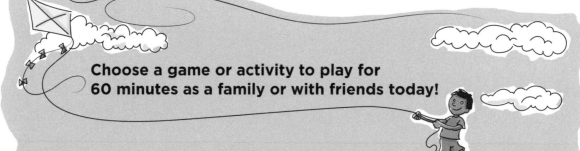

**Choose a game or activity to play for 60 minutes as a family or with friends today!**

## Day 10

## Choose a **Play** or **Exercise** Activity!

# INCENTIVE CONTRACT CALENDAR

My parents and I agree that if I complete this section of

## Summer Fit Activities™

and read _____ minutes a day, my reward will be _____

Child Signature: _____     Parent Signature: _____

| | | | | | |
|---|---|---|---|---|---|
| Day 1 | ✏️ | 📖 | Day 6 | ✏️ | 📖 |
| Day 2 | ✏️ | 📖 | Day 7 | ✏️ | 📖 |
| Day 3 | ✏️ | 📖 | Day 8 | ✏️ | 📖 |
| Day 4 | ✏️ | 📖 | Day 9 | ✏️ | 📖 |
| Day 5 | ✏️ | 📖 | Day 10 | ✏️ | 📖 |

Color the  for each day of activities completed.

Color the  for each day of reading completed.

 Fill in how many exercise days completed _____

 Parents initial at end of each completed section _____

# Summer Explorer
## Discover New Things to Play and Do!

- Learn how to make paper airplanes.

- Host a board game night.

- Play charades.

- Use cardboard boxes to build an outdoor house, fort, train, or pirate ship.

- Play jump rope, marbles, or hopscotch.

- Use "junk" from around your house to create an art masterpiece.

- Make some puppets and put on a puppet show.

- Go through your toys and have a toy exchange or donate to charity.

- Fly a kite.

- Draw with sidewalk or paint with water on the cement.

- Create a new exercise or exercise routine.

- Organize a neighborhood garbage walk to pick up trash and clean up your neighborhood.

- Search for animal tracks. How many can you identify?

- Play in the sand. Build a sand castle.

- Play Frisbee.

- Write a letter to someone and mail it.

- Visit a local nature preserve.

- Make a robot or other creation out of items from your recycle bin.

- Paint a pet rock.

## Recyclable Creations "Junk Monsters"

1 Gather clean cans, bottles, and boxes from recycling bin.

2 Use plastic lids, newspaper strips, nuts, screws, buttons, pipe cleaners, rubber bands to make faces, and arms and legs. Your parents will need to help you glue with a hot glue gun.

3 Create monsters, robots, or your family members!

4-5 • © Summer Fit Activities™

**The Earth**

**Read the passage then answer the questions.**

The earth is about 4,000 miles thick from surface to center. If you could cut open the earth you would see many layers. The outside layer, the layer we see is called the crust and is between 5 and 25 miles thick. This layer is the thinnest layer and is covered with soil, rocks, mountains, and trees.

The next layer is the mantle, and is the largest layer at about 1,800 miles thick. The mantle makes up 85% of the total weight and mass of the earth. As you move through the mantle, the temperatures rise until reaching 3,000 degrees Celsius.

The outer core is about 1,400 miles thick and is made up of super-heated molten lava. At the very center of the earth is the inner core, which is believed to be a solid ball of iron and nickel. This layer is about 800 miles thick.

It is very hot beneath the earth's surface. Magma is molten rock that is found beneath the surface of the earth. Hot magma and gasses collect in pools under pressure that can cause the magma to push up through weak spots on the earth's surface. When this happens a volcano is born. The magma that pushes its way out of the earth's crust is called lava. Sometimes lava oozes or pours out of the earth and sometimes it erupts violently, shooting the lava, ashes, gases, and steam up and out. The lava eventually cools and hardens to form igneous rock.

**Label the layers of the earth.**

| crust | outer core | mantle | inner core |
|---|---|---|---|

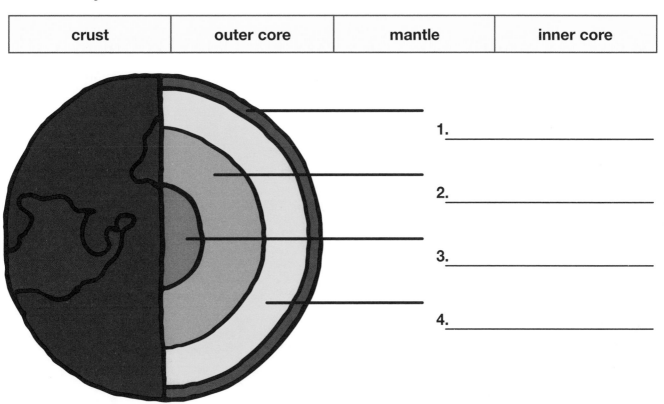

1._____

2._____

3._____

4._____

**Underline the topic sentence for each paragraph.**

## Story Problem

**Read each of the following story problems and solve.**

1. Last year Harry's hot dog stand sold an average of 56 hot dogs on each of the 302 days he was open. How many hot dogs did he sell?

_____

2. There are 24 cans of peaches in each case and 112 cases delivered to the grocery store. How many cans of peaches were delivered?

_____

3. There are 118 passengers on flight 205. Each passenger has 75 pounds of luggage. What is the total weight of the luggage?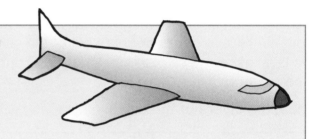

_____

4. The violinist practices 50 minutes each day. How many minutes does she practice in a week?

_____

5. Twenty-eight bags of salt were delivered to the factory. Each bag weighs 50 pounds. How many pounds of salt were delivered?

_____

## Choose your STRENGTH exercise!

Recored in Fitness Log

**Exercise for today:**

_____

**Day 1**

4–5 • © Summer Fit Activities™

 **Vocabulary**

**Read each sentence.  Circle the word that means the same as the underlined word.**

1. The boys <u>giggled</u> through the entire movie.

cried        Ex: (laughed)        complained        danced

2. The man outside the bank was <u>unjustly</u> accused of robbing the bank.

fairly        unfairly        immediately        only

3. The boy <u>intentionally</u> kicked his sister under the table.

accidentally        deliberately        quickly        quietly

4. There was <u>chaos</u> in the classroom when the students realized their pet snake had escaped.

disorder        organization        calm        order

5. The girls were scared when they heard an <u>eerie</u> noise coming from the basement.

loud        interesting        creepy        funny

6. We waited in line to <u>purchase</u> our tickets for the movie.

buy        borrow        sell        find

7. We should hurry so we are not <u>tardy</u> to class.

early        late        quick        walking

Classify each angle as acute, obtuse, or right.

| 1. | 2. | 3. |
|---|---|---|
| _____ | _____ | _____ |

| 4. Draw a 45° angle. Classify the angle. | 5. Draw a 90° angle. Classify the angle. |
|---|---|
| _____ | _____ |

6. Look at the polygon.

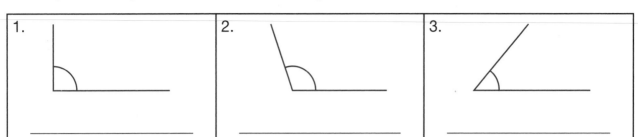

The name of this polygon is _____.

How many obtuse angles? _____     How many acute angles? _____

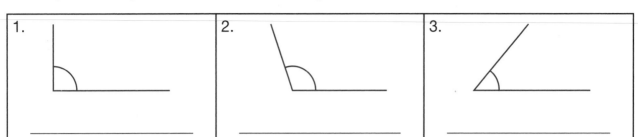

## Choose your AEROBIC exercise!

**Exercise for today:**

_____

Recored in Fitness Log

**Day 2**

## Spiders

**Read the passage on spiders.**
**Then, answer the questions below.**

Although there are few creatures that inspire fear like spiders, they are not really as dangerous as people think. The fact is that you are more likely to die from a bee sting, lightning strike, or snake bite than you are from a spider bite. The black widow and brown recluse are the most dangerous spiders in North America. The black widow is easily recognized by its shiny black body and the red hourglass mark on its abdomen. The brown recluse can be identified by the distinctive violin mark on its back. While there are spiders that are dangerous to humans, most spiders have venom that is only harmful to their natural prey. Because they are hunters, spiders can be found everywhere there is food; in forests, deserts, water, and even your house. The good news is that spiders eat more insects than all other creatures combined. An old English saying says, "If you wish to live and thrive, let the spider stay alive." Too many spiders are killed because of fear or ignorance.

Spiders are cold blooded invertebrates that have exoskeletons. This means they wear their skeleton on the outside. Because of their exoskeleton, all spiders molt, or shed, their skin as they grow. Spiders can have between two and eight pairs of eyes, two main body parts, and four pairs of legs. Spinnerets allow the spider to spin a web made from liquid made in silk glands in the abdomen. While all spiders spin silk, many don't build webs to catch their prey. Some spiders use venom from their fangs to overpower and kill their prey. The spider's jaw and mouth help it to pre-digest its food by injecting its prey with digestive juices. The prey's internal organs and muscles are turned to liquid, and the spider is able to drink its meal. The spider is a fascinating and beneficial creature to have nearby.

> **Play spiders and flies with your friends. One person is the spider. The flies run across the yard without getting tagged. Once tagged, flies become part of the web and can tag others from sitting down. Last one tagged is the new spider.**

**Write true or false.**

1. All spiders are dangerous. _____

2. The brown recluse has a violin shape on its back. _____

3. Spiders are cold-blooded invertebrates. _____

4. All spiders spin webs. _____

5. Spiders eat more insects than any other creature. _____

6. Spiders pre-digest their food. _____

7. Look up the word fascinating in a dictionary and write the definition.

   fascinating: _____

**Subtract to find the answers.**

| 1. | 3. | 5. | 7. | 9. |
|---|---|---|---|---|
| 845<br>− 234 | 724<br>− 356 | 891<br>− 462 | 510<br>- 359 | 205<br>- 187 |

| 2. | 4. | 6. | 8. | 10. |
|---|---|---|---|---|
| 73.71<br>− 19.52 | 53.85<br>− 19.68 | 76.48<br>− 23.59 | 48.98<br>- 36.18 | 32.09<br>− 29.19 |

**Find the area.**

11.

**42 in**

**23 in**

area = _____ squared inches

12.

**98 ft**

**45 ft**

area = _____ squared feet

**Divide to find the answers.**

13. 2 ⟌ 45     14. 5 ⟌ 87     15. 4 ⟌ 59     16. 4 ⟌ 83     17. 2 ⟌ 27

## Choose your STRENGTH exercise!

**Exercise for today:**

**Day 3**

Recored in
Fitness Log

 **Common and Proper Noun**

A common noun names a person, place, thing or idea, such as brother, campground, or boat. A proper noun names a particular person, place, or thing, such as Michael, Camp Rogers, and the Titanic. Proper nouns are names so they are always capitalized. Common nouns are not names so they are not capitalized.

**Write a proper noun for each common noun.**

1. building     Empire State Building.
_____    _____

2. newspaper
_____    _____

3. city
_____    _____

4. street
_____    _____

5. state
_____    _____

6. park
_____    _____

7. ocean
_____    _____

8. book
_____    _____

**Write a common noun for each proper noun.**

9. Target     store
_____    _____

10. Isabella
_____    _____

11. Dodgers
_____    _____

12. Lake Michigan
_____    _____

13. Easter
_____    _____

14. France
_____    _____

15. Toyota
_____    _____

16. Poodle
_____    _____

**Read each sentence. Underline the common nouns and circle the proper nouns.**

17. My family went to France last summer.

18. *Despicable Me* is my favorite movie.

19 We had a picnic at Liberty Park on Memorial Day.

20. I sang "Twinkle, Twinkle, Little Star" to my baby sister, Maddie.

21. My friends, Jacob and Pedro, met me at the corner of Elm Street and Maple Avenue.

22. January can be very cold in Columbus, Ohio.

23. My Basset Hound had six puppies in December.

24. Mrs. Smith is the librarian at our school but Mr. Dean is the librarian at Lincoln Heights.

# Identifying Triangles

Like fractions are fractions with the same denominator. You can add and subtract like fractions easily. Simply add or subtract the numerators and write the sum over the common denominator. Simplify if you can by dividing the numerator and the denominator with the common factor. A common factor is a number that will divide into both numbers evenly.

| | | |
|---|---|---|
| 1. $\dfrac{1}{10} + \dfrac{3}{10} = \dfrac{4}{10}$ | 5. $\dfrac{8}{6} - \dfrac{3}{6} =$ | 9. $\dfrac{16}{20} - \dfrac{12}{20} =$ |
| 2. $\dfrac{4}{8} + \dfrac{3}{8} =$ | 6. $\dfrac{8}{12} - \dfrac{3}{12} =$ | 10. $\dfrac{5}{9} + \dfrac{2}{9} =$ |
| 3. $\dfrac{3}{8} + \dfrac{3}{8} =$ | 7. $\dfrac{12}{16} - \dfrac{9}{16} =$ | 11. $\dfrac{5}{8} + \dfrac{2}{8} =$ |
| 4. $\dfrac{11}{21} + \dfrac{3}{21} =$ | 8. $\dfrac{12}{12} - \dfrac{3}{12} =$ | 12. $\dfrac{15}{20} - \dfrac{10}{20} =$ |

**Reduce each fraction.**

| | | |
|---|---|---|
| 13. Ex: $\dfrac{10}{100} = \dfrac{1}{10}$ | 16. $\dfrac{6}{24} = $ ___ | 19. $\dfrac{8}{20} = $ ___ |
| 14. $\dfrac{5}{25} = $ ___ | 17. $\dfrac{9}{18} = $ ___ | 20. $\dfrac{2}{18} = $ ___ |
| 15. $\dfrac{2}{12} = $ ___ | 18. $\dfrac{12}{14} = $ ___ | 21. $\dfrac{3}{15} = $ ___ |

## Choose your AEROBIC exercise!

**Day 4**

**Exercise for today:**

Recored in Fitness Log

# KINDNESS

Value

*Kindness is being nice and caring about people, animals, and the earth. Kindness is looking for ways to help others before ourselves and going out of our way to let others know that we care.*

**Princess Diana** of Wales was a modern-day princess who will always be admired for her kindness and generosity. Princess Diana gave selflessly to others and worked with many charity organizations that helped people around the world. She visited adults and children in impoverished countries who were sick, homeless, or abandoned and listened to their stories and needs.

Princess Diana used her power and fame to raise awareness for people who had been forgotten and made ordinary people feel extraordinary by simply taking the time to let them know that she cared.

**1.** How did Princess Diana show kindness to others?

_____

_____

_____

**2.** What is an antonym for the word "ordinary"? _____

**3.** What is a synonym for the word "kind"? _____

**4.** Write your definition for kindness. Kindness is _____

_____

_____

# Value:

# KINDNESS

## FAMILY ACTIVITIES

**Choose one or more activities to do with your family or friends.**

 Play "10 good things" with your friends or family. Pick a person and tell 10 nice things about them.

 Write notes to your neighbors thanking them for being good neighbors.

 Have a lemonade stand and donate the money you earn to a food bank or homeless shelter.

 Collect toys, books, and games you no longer play with and donate them.

## VALUES ARE A FAMILY AFFAIR

Read more about
**KINDNESS**

**Crash**
By Jerry Spinelli

**Bullies Are A Pain in the Brain**
By Trevor Romaine

**Joshua T. Bates Takes Charge**
By Susan Shreve

**Choose a game or activity to play for 60 minutes as a family or with friends today!**

## Day 5

## Choose a **Play** or **Exercise** Activity!

# Summer Fitness Log

Choose your exercise activity each day from the Aerobic and Strength Activities in the back of the book. Record the date, stretch, activity and how long you performed your exercise activity below. Fill in how many days you complete your fitness activity on your Incentive Contract Calendars.

| | Date | Stretch | Activity | Time |
|---|---|---|---|---|
| examples: | June 4 | Run in place | Sky Reach | 7 min |
| | June 5 | Toe Touches | Bottle Curls | 15 min |
| 1. | | | | |
| 2. | | | | |
| 3. | | | | |
| 4. | | | | |
| 5. | | | | |
| 6. | | | | |
| 7. | | | | |
| 8. | | | | |
| 9. | | | | |
| 10. | | | | |

I promise to do my best for me. I exercise to be healthy and active. I am awesome because I am me.

Child Signature: _____

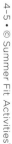

# Summer Journal III

Write about your best friend, brother or sister.

4-5 • © Summer Fit Activities™

**Circle the word(s) in each row that are spelled correctly.**

| | | | | |
|---|---|---|---|---|
| 1. | pased | passet | passed | past |
| 2. | realy | really | reelly | reley |
| 3. | about | abowt | aboat | abot |
| 4. | agen | agaen | again | againe |
| 5. | somtimes | sometimes | sumtimes | sometimez |
| 6. | dosen't | dozen't | doesn't | duesn't |

**Write the correct word for each sentence.**

| their | there | they're |
|---|---|---|

7. _____ dog has fleas.

8. _____ going on vacation Saturday.

9. Put the books on the table over _____.

| right | write |
|---|---|

10. I am going to _____ my thank you notes tomorrow.

11. Turn _____ on Mapleridge Road to get to Washington Park.

**Choose the words that correctly complete the sentence.**

12. I hope (are, our) track team does (good, well) in the regional track (meat, meet).

13. (Whose, Who's) going to be the fourth grade teacher next year?

14. When (are, our) you going to the waterpark?

15. Cold lemonade tastes so (good, well) on a hot day.

The median number is the number that falls in the exact middle of the data set when arranged least to greatest. Give the median of each data set of number.

| | |
|---|---|
| **1.** 20, 10, 40, 30 50, _____ | **4.** 4,8,10, 12, 14, 16, 18 _____ |
| **2.** 120, 145, 156, 168, 176, 188, 190 _____ | **5.** 200, 300, 100, 400, 500 _____ |
| **3.** 4,2,3,6,7,5,9 _____ | **6.** 15, 17, 10, 18, 20 _____ |

To find the **mean**, or average, add the numbers and divide the total by how many numbers are in the set. **Example:** Mean of 4 and 2 is 4 + 2 = 6. 6 ÷ 2 = 3 **Mean = 3**

**1. What is the mean age of the Hernandez children?**

Sam 2, Sally 3, Ann 5, Joseph 7, Gabe 8      Mean = _____

**2. What is the mean of movie ratings for the top 5 movies?**

5, 4, 3, 3, 5      Mean= _____

**3. What is the mean of test scores for Group 1?**

70, 80, 80, 90, and 100      Mean= _____

The mode is the number that occurs most often in a set. Find the mode for each set.

| | |
|---|---|
| **1.** 3, 4 ,5 ,5 ,6 ,7 ,4 ,5<br>Mode = _____ | **3.** 25, 20, 15, 20, 10, 20.<br>Mode = _____ |
| **2.** 12, 10, 13, 10, 14, 15<br>Mode = _____ | **4.** 50, 45, 35, 45, 50, 45.<br>Mode = _____ |

The range is the difference between the greatest and least number in a data set. Find the range for each set.

| | |
|---|---|
| **1.** 1,5,8,6,4,10<br>Range = _____ | **3.** 40, 90, 10, 50, 70, 30, 100<br>Range = _____ |
| **2.** 13, 45, 20 66, 24, 52<br>Range = _____ | **4.** 16, 12, 9, 24, 17, 2, 16, 21<br>Range = _____ |

## Choose your AEROBIC exercise!

**Exercise for today:**

Recored in Fitness Log

**Day**
**6**

**Day 7**

## Reading a Chart

**Use the chart below to answer the questions.**

| State | Capital | Admission Date | Famous Native |
|-------|---------|----------------|---------------|
| Alabama | Montgomery | Dec. 14, 1819 | Helen Keller |
| Georgia | Atlanta | Jan. 2, 1788 | Martin Luther King Jr. |
| Virginia | Richmond | June 25, 1788 | Lewis and Clark |
| Louisiana | Baton Rouge | April 30, 1812 | Louis Armstrong |
| Kansas | Topeka | Jan. 29, 1861 | Amelia Earhart |
| Arizona | Phoenix | Feb. 14, 1912 | Geronimo |

1. What is the capital of Louisiana? _____

2. What two states became a state in the same year? _____,_____.

3. Who is the famous native of Alabama? _____

4. Topeka is the capital of what state?_____

5. What state became a state on Valentine's Day? _____

6. Lewis and Clark came from what state? _____

7. Which capital has four syllables in its name? _____

8. Put the states mentioned in alphabetical order._____,_____,

_____,_____,_____,_____.

9. When did Georgia become a state?_____

10. Which famous native only had one name?_____. What state was he/she from?

_____.

4-5 • © Summer Fit Activities™

SummerFitActivities.com

69

# Multiples

The numbers you say when you skip count are multiples. The first multiple of a number is always the number itself. For example the multiples of 2 are: 2, 4, 6, 8, 10, 12, 14, 16, 18, 20… and so on.

**Find the first 6 multiples for each number.**

1 = _____, _____, _____, _____, _____, _____ .

2 = _____, _____, _____, _____, _____, _____ .

3 = _____, _____, _____, _____, _____, _____ .

**4. Circle the multiples of 8.**

| 10 | 12 | 8 | 23 | 24 | 16 |
|----|----|----|----|----|----|
| 40 | 38 | 48 | 53 | 56 | 64 |
| 72 | 89 | 80 | 90 | 88 | 17 |

**5. Circle the multiples of 5.**

| 6 | 5 | 12 | 15 | 20 | 25 |
|----|----|----|----|----|----|
| 36 | 55 | 45 | 40 | 53 | 60 |
| 73 | 75 | 82 | 90 | 103 | 100 |

**6. Multiples of 3 and 5 (list 5).**

Multiples of 3: _____     Multiples of 5: _____

Least common multiple = _____

7. What is the 5th multiple of 9? _____     8. What is the 8th multiple of 11? _____

9. List 10 multiples of 10: _____,_____,_____,_____,_____,_____,_____,_____,_____,_____ .

## Choose your STRENGTH exercise!

**Exercise for today:**

_____

**Day 7**

Recored in Fitness Log

4–5 • © Summer Fit Activities™

Adjectives modify nouns and answer what kind? Which? How many? Adverbs modify verbs, adjectives, and other adverbs. Adverbs answer the question how? Write whether the underlined word is an adverb or adjective.

1. Mom made my friends and I <u>delicious</u> cookies. _____

2. We worked <u>hard</u> to win the competition. _____

3. It was a <u>rainy</u> day so we decided to play indoors. _____

4. The pianist played <u>beautifully</u> in the recital. _____

5. The fierce shark attacked the <u>helpless</u> seal pup. _____

6. The horse galloped <u>steadily</u> across the field. _____

7. The girls ran <u>quickly</u> to school so they wouldn't be late. _____

8. The <u>fussy</u> baby cried for his mother._____

9. The snake slithered <u>silently</u> under the rock and out of sight. _____

10. Gabriel and Thomas <u>eagerly</u> waited for their turn to try the jet ski._____

**Write the comparative and superlative form of each adjective.**

| adjective | comparative | superlative |
|---|---|---|
| 11. big | bigger | biggest |
| 12. small | _____ | _____ |
| 13. sad | _____ | _____ |
| 14. sleepy | _____ | _____ |
| 15. interesting | _____ | _____ |
| 16. short | _____ | _____ |
| 17. useful | _____ | _____ |
| 18. happy | _____ | _____ |

**Give all the factors of each number.**

Ex. 8 = ___1,2,4,8___ .

**1.** 6 = _____

**4.** 10 = _____

**2.** 12 = _____

**5.** 18 = _____

**3.** 25 = _____

**6.** 16 = _____

**7. Give all the factors of 16 and 24. Circle the greatest common factor (GCF).**

16 : _____

24: _____

**8. Give all the factors of 15 and 30. Circle the GCF.**

15 : _____

30: _____

**Read the following story problems and solve.**

| | | |
|---|---|---|
| **9.** | The performance began at 7:45 p.m. and ended at 10:55 p.m. How long was the play? | _____ hours and _____ minutes |
| **10.** | On Monday, Emily worked on her computer for 8 hours. If she began at 8:00 a.m. what time did she finish? | _____ a.m. or p.m. |
| **11.** | It took Jeremy 6 hours and 15 minutes to paint the garage. If Jeremy finished painting at 3:30 p.m., what time was it when he began painting? | _____ a.m. or p.m. Draw the time he began on the clock.  |

**Choose your AEROBIC exercise!**

**Exercise for today:**

_____

Recored in Fitness Log

**Day**
**8**

4–5 • © Summer Fit Activities™

On April 10, 1912 the Titanic set sail from England on its "maiden" voyage, with 2,200 people aboard.  It took 3,000 men two years to build the Titanic.  The ship was a luxurious floating palace with swimming pools, elegant restaurants, and indoor gardens unlike any other ship of its time. Titanic had a crew of 900 and was powered by pressurized steam from burning coal.  Eleven stories high and 882 feet long, the Titanic was bound for New York City and intended to make record time.  Who could have imagined that its first voyage would be its last?

The builder bragged that the Titanic was unsinkable, and the enormous ship steamed full speed through the calm, dark waters of the Atlantic Ocean.  The crew had been receiving iceberg warnings for a few days, but the moonless night and unusually calm waters made the warning that fateful night come too late.  Although the Titanic tried to maneuver away, the ship hit and the iceberg ripped open a hole nearly 300 feet long in its mighty hull.   Water poured into the lower decks, and the unsinkable Titanic  began to sink.  Because there were not enough lifeboats, only 705 of the 2,200 passengers on board survived, most of them women and children.  Within hours, the largest ship in the world was at the bottom of the Atlantic Ocean.

**Circle the letter of the correct answer.**

| 1. In this passage, the word <u>unsinkable</u> means: | |
|---|---|
| a. buoyant | c. heavy |
| b. enormous | d. light |

| 3. So many passengers died because: | |
|---|---|
| a. there were not enough lifeboats | c. they couldn't swim |
| b. they wanted to stay on board | d. they couldn't see the lifeboats |

| 2. A ships "maiden " voyage is its… | |
|---|---|
| a. longest voyage | c. first voyage |
| b. last voyage | d. shortest voyage |

| 4. If you wanted to learn more about the Titanic you could look in… | |
|---|---|
| a. a dictionary | c. an atlas |
| b. a globe | d. an encyclopedia |

| 5. The builder's attitude about the Titanic can be described as… | | | |
|---|---|---|---|
| a. humble | b. arrogant | c. modest | d. happy |

## Equivalent Measurement

**Fill in the correct number.**

1. 3 weeks = _____ days

2. 2 dozen = _____

3. 180 minutes = _____ hours

4. 3 years = _____months

5. 8 pairs = _____

6. 48 hours = _____ days

7. 36 inches = _____ feet

8. 9 feet = _____ inches

9. 6 hours = _____ minutes

10. 7 days = _____ hours

11. 2 gallons = _____ quarts

12. 120 seconds = _____ minutes

A number line shows the order of numbers. Complete the number lines.

13.

3.0    3.1    3.2    3.3    _____    3.5    3.6    _____

14.

10    20    _____    40    50    _____    70    80    _____    100

15.

3    3 1/4    3 1/2    3 3/4    4    4 1/4    _____    _____    _____    5 1/4    _____    _____    6

**16. Identify the pattern, and then complete the chart.**

| Input | output | |
|-------|--------|---|
| 64 | 8 | |
| 48 | _____ | |
| 16 | _____ | |
| 32 | 4 | Pattern: _____ |
| 80 | _____ | |
| _____ | 5 | |
| 24 | _____ | |

## Choose your STRENGTH exercise!

**Day 9**

**Exercise for today:**

_____

Recored in Fitness Log

4-5 • © Summer Fit Activities™

# COURAGE

*Courage means doing the right thing even when it is difficult and you are afraid. Courage includes being brave and taking a stand.*

On Thursday, December 1, 1955, **Rosa Parks** got on the bus after a long day at work. At that time busses were segregated, which meant that black people and white people were separated because of the color of their skin. Black people were expected to give up their seats to white passengers if a white person was standing. A few stops after Rosa sat down, a white passenger got on the bus. When the bus driver noticed that a white person was standing he called back to the four black people and told them to give up their seats. The other three got up and stood at the back of the bus, but Rosa refused. She had given up her seat before and it was not right, it was not fair. On this day Rosa stood up for what she believed in and did not budge. The police were called and Rosa was arrested. The people in the community were so inspired by Rosa's act of courage that they organized a bus boycott and stopped riding the bus. Finally, the rules for riding the bus were changed and made fair for everyone. Rosa's decision to fight for what she believed in was an important moment in the fight for the civil rights of all African Americans. Rosa is a hero and is considered the Mother of the Civil Rights Movement.

**Circle each courageous act.**

| | |
|---|---|
| Fighting | Walking away from a fight |
| Standing up for someone who is being bullied | Teasing and bullying someone |
| | Blaming others |
| Admitting your mistake | |
| | Doing what is right |
| Following the crowd | |
| | Looking out for yourself |
| Helping others | |
| | Working hard and trying again |
| Quitting when something is difficult | |

# Value:

# COURAGE

## FAMILY ACTIVITIES

**Choose one or more activities to do with your family or friends.**

 As a family, watch a movie that demonstrates courage such as *Charlotte's Web*, *The Sound of Music*, *The Wizard of Oz*, *The Lion King*, *ET*, or *Finding Nemo*. Discuss how the characters in the movie display courage. What might have happened if they hadn't been courageous?

 Make and decorate a pennant for your room that says "I believe in myself." Discuss with your parents how being the best you can be is an act of courage.

 Talk about the courage it takes for a blind person to get through the day. Take turns blindfolding each other and try to do your everyday things. Ask your parents to help you look up the story of Ben Underwood, a blind teen who rides a skateboard and plays video games.

 Think about the most courageous person you know. Write about how they demonstrate courage.

## Let's talk about it...

Courage is something built over time. Discuss everyday situations with your child and the opportunities they have to be brave. Read books about people who display courage. Encourage them to share their fears and brainstorm together ways to face and overcome those fears. Talk with them about a time you were afraid but found the courage to get through.

## VALUES ARE A FAMILY AFFAIR

 Read more about **COURAGE**

**The Boy Who Dared**
By Susan Campbell Bartoletti

**Call It Courage**
By Armstrong Sperry

**Kids with Courage**
By Barbara Leaks

Choose a game or activity to play for **60 minutes as a family or with friends today!**

## Day 10

### Choose a **Play** or **Exercise** Activity!

# INCENTIVE CONTRACT CALENDAR

My parents and I agree that if I complete this section of

and read _____ minutes a day, my reward will be _____

Child Signature: _____     Parent Signature: _____

| | | | | | |
|---|---|---|---|---|---|
| Day 1 | | | Day 6 | | |
| Day 2 | | | Day 7 | | |
| Day 3 | | | Day 8 | | |
| Day 4 | | | Day 9 | | |
| Day 5 | | | Day 10 | | |

 Color the for each day of activities completed.

Color the  for each day of reading completed.

 Fill in how many exercise days completed _____

 Parents initial at end of each completed section _____

# Summer Explorer
## Discover New Things to Play and Do!

- Learn the phases of the moon. Look at it several nights in a row and see if you can recognize the various phases.

- Make up a song or dance.

- Have a yard sale.

- Start a rock collection.

- Have a potluck dinner with family and friends.

- Visit a farmers market. Learn about the origin of the food you eat.

- Volunteer.

- Take a hike.

- Have a neighborhood softball game.

- Make popsicles.

- Grab some binoculars and go on a bird watching hike.

- Go camping.

- Have a western theme night. Wear bandanas and your cowboy boots, and roast hotdogs. Try line dancing or watch an old Western.

- Go on a nature walk. Collect twigs, leaves, pebbles, and shells. Glue them on card stock to make a 3D masterpiece.

- Help a neighbor by mowing their lawn or weeding.

- Draw a comic strip.

- Bake cookies and take some to a friend or neighbor.

- Play Hide and Seek.

- Have a pillow fight.

- Create a time capsule.

## Nature Walk

**1** Go on a nature walk in a field, park or beach

**2** Collect grass, twigs, shells, pebbles, etc.

**3** Arrange your finds inside a cardboard box, glue down to create a 3D masterpiece.

A noun is a word that is used to name a person, place, or thing. Fill in the correct category for each word: person, place, or thing.

1. moon _____ watermelon _____ park _____ pilot _____ boy _____

2. book _____ zoo _____ friend _____ rattle snake _____ rock _____

3. school _____ grandma _____ library _____ water park _____ girl _____

Possessive nouns show ownership and are formed by adding an 's or s' for plurals. Use the nouns above to complete each sentence below.

4. The _____'s most popular animals are the monkeys.

5. The _____'s dog won first place at the dog show.

6. Yesterday, the _____'s new slide opened.

7. My _____'s cookies are delicious.

8. The _____'s dance recital was cancelled.

9. The _____'s attempt to land the plane in the storm was successful.

10. A _____'s bite can be deadly.

A possessive pronoun shows ownership: our, my, his, hers, mine, their ,her, your. Circle the possessive pronoun.

| | | |
|---|---|---|
| 11. My cat is orange. | 14. Our house is white. | 17. That ball is hers. |
| 12. This book is mine. | 15. His dog had puppies. | 18. Is that your bike? |
| 13. Please tie your shoes. | 16. The girl fed her frog. | 19. That is their car. |

## Mixed Practice

**Complete the equation in the parenthesis first. Then solve the problem.**

1. (4 + 5) x 2 = _____

2. (12 + 4) – (7+3) = _____

3. 9 + (4 x 2) = _____

4. 3 ÷ (8 x 9) = _____

5. (5 - 3) x (6 + 2) = _____

6. (12 x 2) -10 = _____

7. (24÷6) + 4 = _____

8. (100 ÷10 ) + 20 = _____

**Round each amount to the nearest dollar.**

9. $2.98 = _____

10. $48.98 = _____

11. $12.89 = _____

12. $51.67 = _____

13. $118.29 = _____

14. $286.51 = _____

**Round each to the nearest dollar and solve.**

15. $56.90 + $42.34 = _____

16. $69.78 + $34.65 = _____

17. $13.89 + $12.12 = _____

18. $129.45 + $115.39 = _____

**Rewrite each number four ways.**

**Ex.** 10 = 5 x 2 =10          2 x 5 =10          10 ÷ 5 = 2          10 ÷ 2 =5

19. 20 = _____, _____, _____, _____

20. 18 = _____, _____, _____, _____

21. 30 = _____, _____, _____, _____

22. 100 = _____, _____, _____, _____

## Choose your STRENGTH exercise!

**Day**
**1**

### Exercise for today:

_____

Recored in
Fitness Log

 **Prefixes**

Adding a prefix to a root word changes the meaning of the word. Read the prefixes and their meanings and answer the questions below.

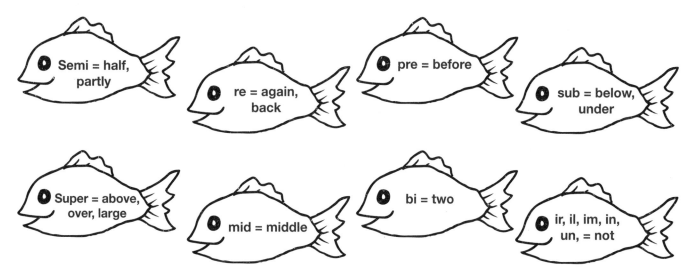

Combine the prefix and root word to make a new word. Write the meaning of the new word.

**Ex:** il + legal = illegal    means: not legal

1. semi + yearly = _____    means _____

2. re + write = _____    means _____

3. pre + order = _____    means _____

4. mid + field = _____    means _____

5. un + clear = _____    means _____

6. super + size = _____    means _____

7. im + possible = _____    means _____

8. ir + regular = _____    means _____

9. bi + cycle = _____    means _____

10. sub + merge = _____    means _____

4-5 • © Summer Fit Activities™

# Rounding and Ordering

**Round each number to the nearest hundred. Ex. 345 =300**

| | | |
|---|---|---|
| 1. 672 _____ | 4. 12,349 _____ | 7. 4,562 _____ |
| 2. 529 _____ | 5. 1,200 _____ | 8. 1,302 _____ |
| 3. 4,355 _____ | 6. 275 _____ | 9. 498 _____ |

**Round each number to the nearest thousand.**

| | | |
|---|---|---|
| 10. 6,709 _____ | 13. 2,302 _____ | 16. 7,943 _____ |
| 11. 5,520 _____ | 14. 16,340 _____ | 17. 112,987 _____ |
| 12. 6,599 _____ | 15. 23,498 _____ | 18. 2,550 _____ |

**Round to the nearest ten-thousand. Ex. 13,989 =10,000**

| | | |
|---|---|---|
| 19. 32,491 _____ | 22. 58,390 _____ | 25. 20,439 _____ |
| 20. 54,376 _____ | 23. 76,890 _____ | 26. 11,209 _____ |
| 21. 143,762 _____ | 24. 267,989 _____ | 27. 531,836 _____ |

**Write these numbers in order from least to greatest.**

1.  1,254        245        2,450        252        21,652

_____, _____, _____, _____, _____.

2.  10,500        5,095        51,501        15,657        595

_____, _____, _____, _____, _____.

3.  909,000        999,023        919,001        19,799        99,198

_____, _____, _____, _____, _____.

## Choose your AEROBIC exercise!

**Exercise for today:**

_____

Recored in
Fitness Log

**Day 2**

## Suffixes - Prefixes

A prefix is a word you put in front of a root word. A suffix is a word you put at the end of a root word. Look at each root word and use the suffixes and prefixes to make as many new words as you can.

ment, able, ed

**Enjoy = enjoyable, enjoyment, enjoyed.**

1. friend (ly, un, ship, less ,be) _____

2. faith (ful, fully, un) _____

3. correct (ed, in, ly) _____

4. complete (ed, ing, tion, ly) _____

5. cook (ing, ed, er, un) _____

6. act (tion, ing, ed, re) _____

**Create five sentences using new words from above. Write them on a separate piece of paper in your best hand writing.**

**Circle the suffix in each word and write the root word on the line.**

7. kindness _____

8. navigation _____

9. courageously _____

10. celebration _____

11. completion _____

12. weakness _____

13. legislator _____

14. shyness _____

15. fruity _____

16. announcer _____

**Classify each pair of lines as parallel, intersecting, or perpendicular.**

1.

_____

_____

_____

2.

_____

_____

3.

_____

_____

| 4. Draw and label a ray. | 5. Draw and label a line segment AB. |
|---|---|
| _____ | _____ |

**6. Name the shape.     How many parallel sides does this shape have?**

Name _____

How many ?_____

**7. Name and describe the polygon.**

The name of this shape is _____.

It has _____ obtuse angles and _____ acute angles.

Choose your **STRENGTH** exercise!

**Day**
**3**

**Exercise for today:**

_____

Recored in Fitness Log

## Cause and Effect Sentences

Some sentences are cause-and-effect sentences. The cause is the reason something happens, and the effect is what happens as a result of the cause.

| Cause and effect sentences often include words like "so", "because" and "and." |
|---|
| Ex. There was a big snowstorm today so school was cancelled. |

| Cause: | Effect: |
|---|---|
| a big snowstorm | school was cancelled |

**Add an effect of the cause in each sentence.**

1. Molly forgot to take the cupcakes out of the oven so, _____

_____ .

2. I woke up late this morning because _____

_____ .

3. The movie was sold out so my friends and I_____

_____ .

4. The gate was left open last night and my dog  _____

_____ .

**Write a cause for the effect in each sentence.**

5. _____

_____ and broke the window.

6. Because I _____

_____ , I was grounded for the weekend.

7. _____

_____ so I had to change my shirt.

8. _____

_____ and had to pay to replace it.

4–5 • © Summer Fit Activities™

**Times tables practice.**

| x | 5 | 6 | 7 |
|---|---|---|---|
| 3 | 15 | 18 | 21 |
| 4 | 20 | 24 | 28 |
| 5 | 25 | 30 | 35 |

| 1. x | 2 | 3 | 4 |
|---|---|---|---|
| 5 | | | |
| 6 | | | |
| 7 | | | |

| 2. x | 3 | 5 | 8 |
|---|---|---|---|
| 2 | | | |
| 7 | | | |
| 0 | | | |
| 6 | | | |
| 4 | | | |

| 3. x | 7 | 8 | 9 |
|---|---|---|---|
| 3 | | | |
| 6 | | | |
| 7 | | | |
| 8 | | | |
| 9 | | | |

4. What time will it be in 1 hour and 15 minutes?

_____

**Write each number in standard form.**

5. 1,000,000 + 200,000 + 60,000 + 5,000 + 400 + 20 + 9 _____

6. 2,000,000 + 300,000 + 40,000 + 7,000 + 80 + 3 _____

7. 500,000 + 70,000 + 3,000 + 600 + 50 + 2 _____

## Choose your **AEROBIC** exercise!

**Exercise for today:**

_____

Recored in
Fitness Log

**Day 4**

4-5 • © Summer Fit Activities™

# RESPECT

*Respect is being nice to yourself and others. Respect includes behaving in a way that makes life safe and peaceful for others even though they may be different than you.*

**Mahatma Gandhi** was a great political and spiritual leader of India. His name means "Great Soul," and he demonstrated that true strength comes from peace and harmony. For years he helped people in India stand up against unfair treatment. His "weapons" were peaceful protests, marches, and strikes. Gandhi believed that every life was valuable and worthy of respect, and he worked hard to protect the rights of all people.

Gandhi taught that if you hurt another person, you also hurt yourself. He wanted people to find peaceful ways of reconciling their differences and to live in harmony with respect for all, even their enemies. Gandhi helped India gain independence by using non-violent means and is considered to be "The Father of the Nation."

**Fill in the blanks using words from the story above.**

**1.** Mahatma Gandhi was a leader of _____ .

**2.** He believed that every life was _____ and worthy of

_____ .

**3.** Gandhi taught that if you hurt others you hurt _____ .

**4.** He inspired people to resolve conflicts _____ .

**5.** List the names of three people who you feel show respect to others.

_____     _____

_____

# Value: RESPECT

Respect is showing good manners and acceptance of other people and our planet. Respect is celebrating differences in culture, ideas and experiences that are different than yours. Respect is accepting that others have lessons to teach us because of their experiences.

"Be the change you want to see in the world."

- Mahatma Gandhi

**List 3 ways to show respect to your parents and teachers.**

**1** _____

**2** _____

**3** _____

**We can disrespect people with our words. Remember to THINK before we speak. Ask yourself...**

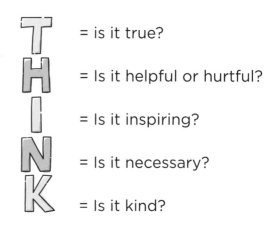

**T** = is it true?

**H** = Is it helpful or hurtful?

**I** = Is it inspiring?

**N** = Is it necessary?

**K** = Is it kind?

## WAYS TO SHOW RESPECT

Respect the Earth.
Collect items to recycle.

Respect a different culture:
Listen to some music or try a new food that is associated with a culture or belief that is different than yours.

**Day 5**

## Choose a Play or Exercise Activity!

# Summer Fitness Log

Choose your exercise activity each day from the Aerobic and Strength Activities in the back of the book. Record the date, stretch, activity and how long you performed your exercise activity below. Fill in how many days you complete your fitness activity on your Incentive Contract Calendars.

| | Date | Stretch | Activity | Time |
|---|---|---|---|---|
| examples: | June 4 | Run in place | Sky Reach | 7 min |
| | June 5 | Toe Touches | Bottle Curls | 15 min |
| 1. | | | | |
| 2. | | | | |
| 3. | | | | |
| 4. | | | | |
| 5. | | | | |
| 6. | | | | |
| 7. | | | | |
| 8. | | | | |
| 9. | | | | |
| 10. | | | | |

I promise to do my best for me. I exercise to be healthy and active. I am awesome because I am me.

Child Signature: _____

# Summer Journal IV

Write about your best summer day so far.

4-5 • © Summer Fit Activities™

 **Can you See Me?**

**Read the passage. Then, answer the questions.**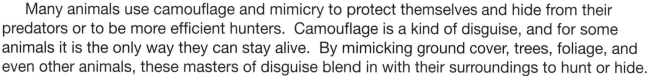

# "Can You See Me?"

Many animals use camouflage and mimicry to protect themselves and hide from their predators or to be more efficient hunters. Camouflage is a kind of disguise, and for some animals it is the only way they can stay alive. By mimicking ground cover, trees, foliage, and even other animals, these masters of disguise blend in with their surroundings to hunt or hide.

Animals can use camouflage in many different ways. Some moths and caterpillars have spots and markings that make them look like the eyes of a much larger animal. Other moths and insects have markings that help them blend in with the bark or leaves of a tree. Stick insects look just like twigs, which allows them to disappear completely and keeps them out of the beak of a hungry bird. Polar bears and the snowy owl are white to blend in with their arctic environment. Animals in the desert tend to be sand colored to blend in with their surroundings. Other animals use the color, shape, and pattern of their skin or fur to blend in with leaves or brush of their environment as well as to successfully hunt for food. For example, the cheetah's spots keep it hidden while it stalks its prey in the savannah grasslands. The chameleon has mastered the art of camouflage and can change its color over and over again to match its surroundings.

**The word camouflage means to conceal or hide. How many smaller words can you find hidden in the word   c a m o u f l a g e?**

| 2 letter words | 3 letter words | 4 letter words | 5 letter words |
|---|---|---|---|
| _____ | _____ | _____ | _____ |
| _____ | _____ | _____ | _____ |
| _____ | _____ | _____ | _____ |
| _____ | _____ | _____ | _____ |

Probability tells how likely an event is to happen. There are six faces on a die. What is the probability that an even number will be rolled?

**Probability = 3/6, 1/2 or 50%**

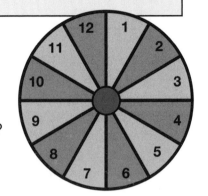

1. Look at the spinner with numbers 1-12.

What is the probability that the spinner will land on a 12?

Probability = _____

2. Look at the die. What is the probability that a 6 will be rolled?

Probability = _____

**Find the coordinates.**

3. What are the coordinates for each point?

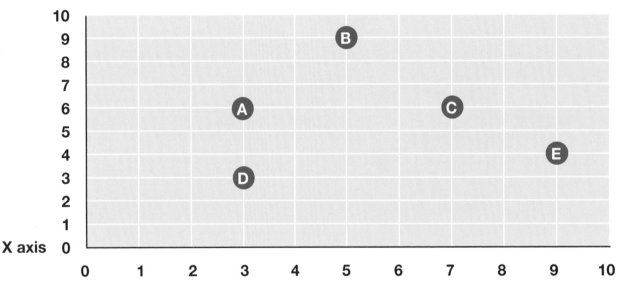

**Y axis**

**X axis**

A = _____  B = _____  C = _____ D = _____ E = _____

Plot the coordinates (2,8) Name this point F.

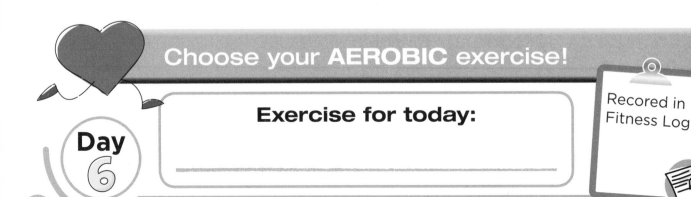

## Choose your **AEROBIC** exercise!

**Exercise for today:**

Recored in
Fitness Log

**Day 6**

## The very Best Pizza

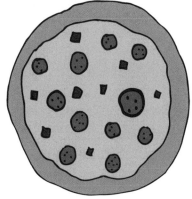

Mimi makes the best pizzas.  First, she follows a recipe to make the pizza dough.  Once the dough is ready, she rolls it out with a rolling pin and puts it on the baking sheet.  Next, she spreads the pizza sauce and sprinkles cheese all over the pizza.  Then she adds her favorite toppings: pepperoni, sausage, and black olives.  Mimi bakes the pizza, and when it cools she cuts it into slices.  Finally, the pizza is ready to eat, delicious!

**Write the steps Mimi takes to make her pizza.**

1. _____

2. _____

3. _____

4. _____

5. _____

6. _____

**7. Think of something you know how to do well.  Write a paragraph that explains how to do it.  Use words such as first, then, next, and finally.**

_____

_____

_____

_____

_____

_____

_____

_____

_____

_____

_____

_____

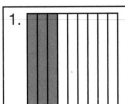

## Mixed Practice with Fractions

**Write the fraction that names the shaded part.**

| 1. | 2. | 3. |
|---|---|---|
| _____ | _____ | _____ |

**Add or subtract. Simplify the answer.**

4.
$$6 \frac{9}{12}$$
$$-2 \frac{3}{12}$$

5.
$$4 \frac{2}{6}$$
$$+2 \frac{4}{6}$$

6.
$$6 \frac{7}{8}$$
$$-2 \frac{3}{8}$$

7. Draw a picture to show 1 2/3.

**Write each fraction as a decimal.**

| 1. 25/100 = _____ | 3. 5/10 = _____ | 5. 7/10 = _____ | 7. 85/100 = _____ |
|---|---|---|---|
| 2. 13/100 = _____ | 4. 50/100 = _____ | 6. 8/10 = _____ | 8. 33/100 = _____ |

**Multiply. Simplify if needed.**

| 9. 2 x 3/4 = _____ | 10. 3 x 4/8 = _____ | 11. 4 x 1/8 = _____ | 12. 6 x 2/18 = _____ |
|---|---|---|---|

**13. Put the fractions in order from least to greatest.**

2/7   4/8   2/3   2/8 = _____

**Compare each set using <,>,or =.**

| 14. 1/2 _____ 2/4 | 15. 0.07 _____ 7/100 | 16. 3/4 _____ 2/3 |
|---|---|---|
| 17. 2/3 _____ 1/3 | 18. 2.45 _____ 2 1/2 | 19. 4/12 _____ 1/3 |
| 20. 3/4 _____ 6/8 | 21. 1 _____ 0.75 | 22. 2/6 _____ 1/12 |

## Choose your STRENGTH exercise!

**Exercise for today:**

_____

Recored in
Fitness Log

Day
7

4-5 • © Summer Fit Activities™

**Day 8**

**Sentence Practice**

A sentence fragment is a group of words that does not express a complete thought.
Write S for each phrase that is a sentence and F for each fragment.

1. _____ Every boy on the team.

2. _____ The dog jumped the fence and ran away.

3. _____ The ball.

4. _____ Wait quietly.

5. _____ Sam finished his homework and went to bed.

6. _____ Screamed loudly.

7. _____ We made cookies for our new neighbors.

8. _____ Parents went.

---

A conjunction is a part of speech that connects two words,
sentences, phrases, or clauses together.

Common conjunctions are: and, but, or, and so.

---

Use a conjunction to combine each set of sentence into one sentence.

Ex. The boy rode his bike.  The boy delivered newspapers.
The boy rode his bike and delivered newspapers.

9. We watered our garden. The plants grew quickly.

_____

10. Anne goes to ballet every Saturday. Joy goes to ballet every Monday.

_____

11. Michael took his canoe to the lake.  Michael took his canoe to go fishing at the lake.

_____

12. Noah could choose chocolate ice cream.  Noah could choose vanilla ice cream.

_____

**Write the name of each kind of angle.**

| obtuse angle An angle 90-180 degrees. | right angle 90 degree angle | acute angle Less than 90 degrees. | straight straight line, no angle. |
|---|---|---|---|

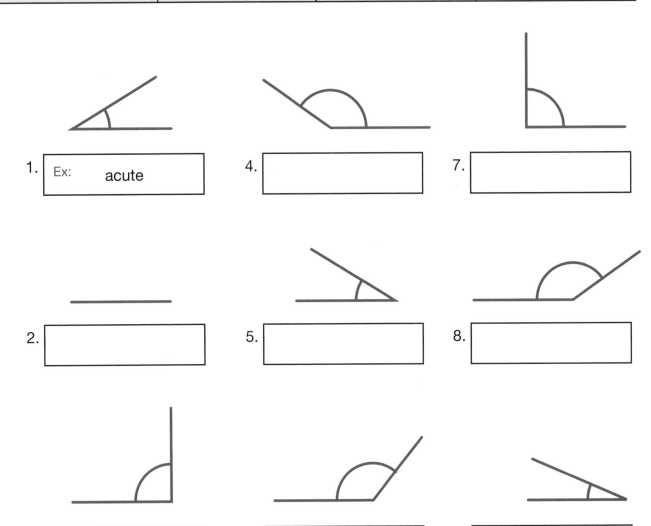

1. Ex: acute

2. 

3. 

4. 

5. 

6. 

7. 

8. 

9. 

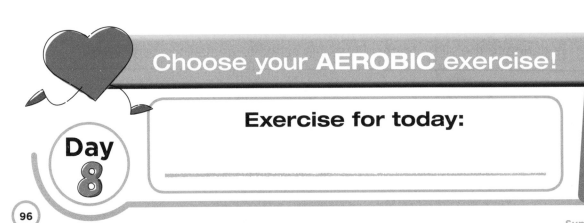

**Choose your AEROBIC exercise!**

**Exercise for today:**

Recored in Fitness Log

**Day 8**

4-5 • © Summer Fit Activities™

## Analogies

An analogy is a similarity between like features of two different things.
Fill in the missing word for each analogy.

1. **Ex.** Tall is to short as fat is to _____ **Thin** _____

2. Boat is to water as airplane is to _____

3. Apple is to fruit as carrot is to _____

4. Moon is to night as sun is to _____

5. Days are to week as months are to _____

6. Up is to down as in is to _____

7. Smile is to happy as frown is to _____

8. Rock is to hard as feather is to _____

9. Cat is to kitten as dog is to _____

10. Fish is to water as bird is to _____

11. Fingers are to hand as toes are to _____

12. Club is to golf as bat is to _____

13. Fire is to hot as ice is to _____

14. Fall is to winter as spring is to _____

**Write your own two analogies.**

15. _____

16. _____

 **Area**

Figures or shapes that have the same shape and size are called congruent figures.

Write "congruent" or "not congruent" underneath the shapes.

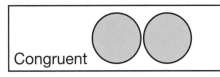 Congruent

 Not congruent

1.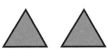

2.

3.

4.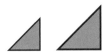

5.

6.

**Draw a congruent figure to match.**

7.

8.

**9. Draw two congruent shapes.**

 Choose your **STRENGTH** exercise!

**Exercise for today:**

 **Day 9**

Recored in Fitness Log

4-5 • © Summer Fit Activities™

Value

*Responsibility is to do what you think you should, for yourself and others, even when it is difficult. When you are responsible people can count on you.*

**Terrance Stanley Fox** was an athlete from Canada. His favorite sport was basketball, but he also played rugby, golf, and ran cross-country in high school. Terry had to have one of his legs amputated after he was diagnosed with cancer. Terry felt that it was his responsibility to make a difference in the lives of others who also had cancer by raising money for cancer research. Even though it would be very difficult for him to do, he decided to run across Canada with an artificial leg to raise money. He called his run the Marathon of Hope. When he started to run in 1980 not many people knew about Terry or what he was doing, but today millions of people all over the world participate or take part in an event named after Terry to raise money for cancer research. The annual Terry Fox Run has become the world's largest one-day fund raiser for cancer research. Terry Fox is considered by many Canadians to be a national hero because he has positively impacted millions of lives around the world.

Terrance Stanley Fox is a hero of responsibility because he did what he had to do for himself and others even though it was difficult to do.

**Number these sentences from the story in the correct order.**

_____ Terry started running in 1980 to raise money for cancer research.

_____ The run has become one of the largest one-day fundraisers for cancer in the world.

_____ Terry played basketball and ran cross-country in high school.

_____ Terry felt it was his responsibility to make a difference and help others who had cancer too.

_____ Terry had to have one of his legs amputated after he was diagnosed with cancer.

_____ Terry named his run "Marathon of Hope."

_____ Terry decided to run across Canada with an artificial leg.

# Value: RESPONSIBILITY

You can show responsibility in many different ways. From doing your homework to babysitting your little brother or sister to helping someone else who is in need, being responsible is being accountable for your actions. Big and small, choosing what you do with your time and efforts is an important part of being responsible.

> "I am not doing the run to become rich or famous."
>
> - Terry Fox, *Marathon of Hope*

| | |
|---|---|
| Monday | |
| Tuesday | |
| Wednesday | |
| Thursday | |
| Friday | |
| Saturday | |
| Sunday | |

**Build or set up a bird feeder in your yard and be responsible for feeding the birds. Use the chart below to track how many birds you feed for a week.**

We are all responsible for the environment. Watch one of these family movies and talk about how being irresponsible can affect the environment. Movies: *Over the Hedge, Hoot, Free Willy, Bambi, Fern Gully, The Last Rainforest,* or *Happy Feet.*

**Day 10**

## Choose a **Play** or **Exercise** Activity!

# INCENTIVE CONTRACT CALENDAR

My parents and I agree that if I complete this section of

and read _____ minutes a day, my reward will be _____

Child Signature: _____     Parent Signature: _____

| | | | | | |
|---|---|---|---|---|---|
| Day 1 | ✏️ | 📖 | Day 6 | ✏️ | 📖 |
| Day 2 | ✏️ | 📖 | Day 7 | ✏️ | 📖 |
| Day 3 | ✏️ | 📖 | Day 8 | ✏️ | 📖 |
| Day 4 | ✏️ | 📖 | Day 9 | ✏️ | 📖 |
| Day 5 | ✏️ | 📖 | Day 10 | ✏️ | 📖 |

Color the  for each day of activities completed.

Color the  for each day of reading completed.

 Fill in how many exercise days completed _____

 Parents initial at end of each completed section _____

# Summer Explorer
## Discover New Things to Play and Do!

- Make up a secret handshake.

- Play "I spy."

- Write a poem.

- Make a telescope out of paper towel tubes. Have a family stargazing night: How many constellations can you find? Can you find the Big Dipper? Polaris?

- Do a puzzle.

- Make ice cream.

- Make a friendship bracelet and give it to a friend.

- Learn to fold Origami.

- Go fishing.

- Camp in the backyard.

- Learn how to juggle.

- Feed the ducks.

- Turn on some music and dance.

- Hang butcher paper on a wall and paint a mural.

- Learn the alphabet in sign language.

- Learn Pig Latin.

- Host a tea party.

- Have a Super Hero Day - dress like your favorite super hero or make up your own. Dress up your pet!

- Walk a dog.

- Do a science experiment.

- Pretend you are a reporter. Interview someone special and write an article about him/her.

## Stargazing

1 Collect paper towel tubes.

2 Gather your family on a clear night to stargaze through your "telescopes."

3 Look for The Big Dipper, Cancer and other star constellations.

 **Antonymns**

Antonyms are words that mean the opposite of other words

Read each phrase. Choose an antonym for the underlined word and circle it.

Example: The antonym of hot is cold.

| | | | | |
|---|---|---|---|---|
| 1. narrow path : | thin | wide | rocky | high |
| 2. water trickled out: | streamed | gushed | leaked | dripped |
| 3. solemn occasion: | serious | sad | happy | special |
| 4. thorough search: | good | incomplete | complete | careful |
| 5. valuable jewelry: | worthless | expensive | fancy | nice |
| 6. talk rapidly: | quickly | quietly | slowly | loudly |
| 7. accept the award: | take | reject | give | receive |
| 8. fierce lion: | mean | scary | loud | gentle |
| 9. unseen complications: | visible | hidden | unexpected | cloudy |

**Write an antonym for each word.**

10. fantasy _____

11. takeoff _____

12. rough _____

13. float _____

14. brief _____

15. harmless _____

4-5 • © Summer Fit Activities™

The line of symmetry is the imaginary line you can use to fold the image in half.

Draw the line of symmetry for each figure. There may be one or more than one.

1.

2.

3.

4.

5.

6.

7.

8.

9.

10.

**11. Which letter does not have a line of symmetry? Circle your answer.**

T          X          Q          O          A

**12. Circle the word below which has a letter that does not have a line of symmetry.**

ABOUT                COT                MOTH                BALD

 **Choose your STRENGTH exercise!**

**Exercise for today:**

_____

Recored in Fitness Log

 **Day 1**

## Amelia Earhart

**Read the passage. Then, answer the questions.**

Amelia Mary Earhart was born on July 24,1897. Amelia went to college in Canada but dropped out to become a volunteer nurse helping the soldiers wounded in World War I. She later taught English to foreign students. Amelia enjoyed watching airshows, and one day after taking a ten minute airplane ride she decided that flying was her vocation. In 1921, Amelia began taking flying lessons and bought her first plane that summer.

In 1932, Amelia became the first woman passenger to fly across the Atlantic Ocean. She later became the first woman pilot to fly the difficult route from California to Hawaii. During her short aviation career, Amelia broke many flying and speed records. In June of 1937, Amelia Earhart and her navigator, Fred Noonan, along with two others, set off from Miami to fly around the world. This was to be her final flight. On July 2, 1937, from somewhere over the Pacific Ocean, a final radio transmission was received. The American Coast Guard lost contact, and Amelia and her crew were never heard from again. After an extensive search, the plane was never found, and the events of that fateful flight remain a mystery.

1. Amelia Earhart was the first woman to fly across the _____

2. Unscramble the words from the story.    taigvnaro _____

anaCda _____

yertysm_____

3. In this story <u>fateful</u> means:    doomed    planned    sad    long

4. Write a couple of sentences stating what you think happened to Amelia Earhart's plane.

_____

_____

_____

_____

**To Try: With your parents permission, download paper airplane templates from the website: www.funpaperairplanes.com**

| | | |
|---|---|---|
| 1. 50 years = _____ decades | 3. 120 months = _____ years | 5. 35 days = _____ weeks |
| 2. _____ centuries = _____ years | 4. 10 decades = _____ years | 6. 3 years = _____ months |

**Fill in the blanks with weeks, years, months, days, or century.**

7. The invention of the light bulb is over one _____ old.

8. My birthday is in four _____ or one_____ .

9. I will be eleven _____ old.

10. Today is Saturday, in three _____ it will be Tuesday.

| 12 inches = 1 foot | 3 feet = 1 yard | 5,280 feet = 1 mile | 1,760 yards = 1 mile |
|---|---|---|---|

**Convert each measurement.**

| | |
|---|---|
| 11. 12 feet = _____ yards | 14. 31,680 feet = _____ miles |
| 12. 6 yards = _____ feet | 15. 3,520 yards = _____ miles |
| 13. 4 miles = _____ feet | 16. 4. 5 feet = _____ inches |

**Use the tables to convert the measurement.**

17.

| Weeks | Days |
|---|---|
| 7 | _____ |
| 4 | _____ |
| _____ | 56 |
| _____ | 14 |

18.

| Hours | Minutes |
|---|---|
| 10 | _____ |
| _____ | 60 |
| _____ | 120 |
| 24 | _____ |

## Choose your AEROBIC exercise!

**Exercise for today:**

_____

**Day 2**

Recored in Fitness Log

4-5 • © Summer Fit Activities™

## Limerick

**A limerick is a humorous and usually nonsensical poem with five lines. Edward Lear (1812-1888) is the British author who is responsible for making limericks popular.**

There once was a man named "Big Pete"
In three steps he could get down the street.
Finding shoes was a chore
For there wasn't a store
That could manage to cover his feet

**Rules of writing a limerick:**

- 5 lines

- The first line often begins "There once was a …" or "There was a …."

- Lines 1, 2 and 5 have 8 or 9 syllables each and rhyme.

- Lines 3 and 4 have 5 or 6 syllables each and rhyme.

**Write a limerick about your family, friends, or a fictional character, illustrate your limerick.**

Write each answer. Ex. 14 x 10 = 140      60 ÷ 10 = 6

| | | |
|---|---|---|
| 1. 56 x 10 = _____ | 4. 158 x 10 = _____ | 7. 279 x 10 = _____ |
| 2. 62 x 10 = _____ | 5. 246 x 10 = _____ | 8. 537 x 10 = _____ |
| 3. 98 x 10 = _____ | 6. 114 x 10 = _____ | 9. 435 x 10 = _____ |

**Divide.**

| | | |
|---|---|---|
| 10. 50 ÷ 10 = _____ | 13. 120 ÷ 10 = _____ | 16. 85 ÷ 10 = _____ |
| 11. 70 ÷ 10 = _____ | 14. 410 ÷ 10 = _____ | 17. 970 ÷ 10 = _____ |
| 12. 100 ÷ 10 = _____ | 15. 780 ÷ 10 = _____ | 18. 230 ÷ 10 = _____ |

**Fill in the blanks.**

| | |
|---|---|
| 19. _____ x 20 = 560 | 23. 83 x _____ = 830 |
| 20. 74 _____ 10 = 740 | 24. _____ x 10 = 5,720 |
| 21. _____ x 10 = 3,560 | 25. _____ ÷10 = 93 |
| 22. _____ ÷ 10 = 63 | 26. _____ x 10 = 4,020 |

27. Circle the multiples of 10.

20    15    30    50    25    100    90    57

| 28. The bakery baked 300 donuts.  If 10 donuts go in each box, how many boxes of donuts will they have? | _____ |
|---|---|

## Choose your STRENGTH exercise!

**Exercise for today:**

_____

Recored in
Fitness Log

Day
3

Persuasive writing is used to try to convince the reader of your ideas. The steps in persuasive writing are to 1) write your opinion 2) give facts or reasons for your opinion and 3) give examples. It is important to brainstorm, organize your thoughts, have a main idea that you back up with details, and end with a strong conclusion.

**Your school has decided to get rid of recess for 5th graders next year. Write a persuasive argument trying to convince the principal to reinstate recess.**

_____

_____

_____

_____

_____

_____

_____

_____

_____

_____

_____

_____

_____

Volume is the amount of space inside a shape. To find the volume multiply the length by the width by the height. **V = l x w x h**

**Ex.** 5 x 3 x 2 = 30 cubic inches

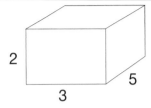

**Find the volume.**

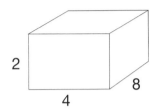

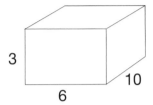

1. volume = _____ cubic inches

2. volume= _____ cubic inches

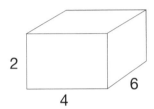

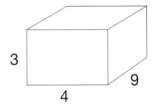

3. volume = _____ cubic inches

4. volume = _____ cubic inches

The volume of Jane's tub is 24 cubic feet. If the length of the tub is 6 feet and the width is 2 feet, what is the height?

5. _____

**Day 4**

Choose your **AEROBIC** exercise!

**Exercise for today:**

Recored in Fitness Log

4-5 • © Summer Fit Activities™

110

SummerFitActivities.com

# PERSEVERANCE

Value

Perseverance

***Perseverance is not giving up or giving in when things are difficult.***

Shark Attack! **Bethany Hamilton** was sitting on her surfboard one sunny day in Hawaii, waiting for the next big wave. Before she knew what happened, a tiger shark attacked. Thirteen-year old Bethany lost one of her arms and nearly died. Not only did she survive, but she was soon back in the water and surfing once again. Bethany had to overcome her fear of another shark attack and had to teach herself how to swim with only one arm. Little by little, against all odds, Bethany was soon competing in and winning surfing competitions.

**Name two things Bethany had to do to persevere and surf again. Bethany had to:**

1._____

2. _____

3. Write about an instance when you had to persevere to overcome something like a challenge or fear. Include what you did to show perseverance and what the outcome was.

_____

_____

_____

_____

_____

_____

_____

# Value: PERSEVERANCE

## FAMILY ACTIVITIES

**Choose one or more activities to do with your family or friends.**

 As a family, tackle a big job you have been putting off such as cleaning the garage or painting the fence. Work together as a family to persevere and finish the job. Celebrate with ice cream to emphasize the sweet satisfaction of a job well done.

 People with disabilities face many obstacles each day. Read about Helen Keller and her perseverance in overcoming her blindness and deafness. Put on a blindfold and imagine how hard it would be to go about your day without your sight. What can you do? What can't you do?

 Farmers need perseverance and a lot of patience when planting their crops. One bad storm or drought can destroy everything they have worked for. Plant a small vegetable garden and take care of weeding and watering it. Be patient and your perseverance will pay off.

### Let's talk about it...

Talk with your child about what perseverance is and why it's important. Discuss the importance of not giving up and sticking with something until it is complete. Lead by example and point out something you are involved in that is difficult and share with he/she how and why you are going to finish.

## VALUES ARE A FAMILY AFFAIR

 Read more about **PERSEVERANCE**

**Fly, Eagle, Fly**
By Desmond Tuto

**I Knew You Could**
By Wally Piper

**Strawberry Girl**
By Lois Lenski

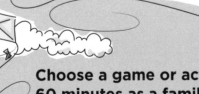

**Choose a game or activity to play for 60 minutes as a family or with friends today!**

## Day 5
### Choose a **Play** or **Exercise** Activity!

# Summer Fitness Log

Choose your exercise activity each day from the Aerobic and Strength Activities in the back of the book. Record the date, stretch, activity and how long you performed your exercise activity below. Fill in how many days you complete your fitness activity on your Incentive Contract Calendars.

| | Date | Stretch | Activity | Time |
|---|---|---|---|---|
| examples: | June 4 | Run in place | Sky Reach | 7 min |
| | June 5 | Toe Touches | Bottle Curls | 15 min |
| 1. | | | | |
| 2. | | | | |
| 3. | | | | |
| 4. | | | | |
| 5. | | | | |
| 6. | | | | |
| 7. | | | | |
| 8. | | | | |
| 9. | | | | |
| 10. | | | | |

I promise to do my best for me. I exercise to be healthy and active. I am awesome because I am me.

Child Signature: _____

# Summer Journal V

Write about your favorite pet or animal.

4-5 • © Summer Fit Activities™

# Go Figure!

**Figurative Language**

**Figurative language can enhance your writing by adding interesting details or painting a vivid picture.**

**Simile**: uses "like" or "as" and makes a comparison using two unlike things.

**Metaphor**: Makes a comparison between two unlike things without using "like" or "as."

**Personification**: Gives human characteristics to non-human things.

**Hyperbole**: Is an exaggeration.

| Label each figure of speech. | | | |
|---|---|---|---|
| Simile = S | Metaphor = M | Personification = P | Hyperbole = H |

1. I'm so hungry I could eat a horse. _____

2. Mom is a stick in the mud when it comes to staying up late. _____

3. The bees played hide and seek in the flowers. _____

4. The math test was as easy as pie. _____

5. My dad snores louder than a freight train. _____

6. The moon smiled down at us. _____

7. My brothers fight like cats and dogs. _____

8. Life is a rollercoaster, so hang on. _____

9. The tree moaned as I hung from its branch. _____

10. The librarian has a heart of stone. _____

11. My sister laughs like a hyena. _____

# Money Matters

| Round each to the nearest dollar. | | Round to the nearest ten dollars. | |
|---|---|---|---|
| 1. $8.67 = _____ | 3. $27.50 = _____ | 5. $31.89 = _____ | 7. $12.86 = _____ |
| 2. $15.30 = _____ | 4. $2.75 = _____ | 6. $52.79 = _____ | 8. $65.42 = _____ |

**Round each to the nearest hundred dollars.**

9. $405.12 = _____   10. $367.96 = _____   11. $650.87 = _____   12. $449.99 = _____

**Round to the leading digit and estimate the sums and differences**
**$41.00 + $37.00 = $80.00.**

| 13. | $35.21 | 14. | $68.98 | 15. | $195.57 | 16. | $529.65 |
|---|---|---|---|---|---|---|---|
| | + $28.67 | | - $ 42.39 | | - $ 117.99 | | + $276.00 |

**17. George earns $72,500 a year, Sam earns $68,489 a year, Max earns $39,752 a year. How much do they earn together?** _____

**Adding, subtracting, and dividing with decimal numbers.**

| 18. | 460.87 | 19. | 678.20 | 20. | $5 \overline{)5.67}$ | 21. | $3 \overline{)9.72}$ |
|---|---|---|---|---|---|---|---|
| | + 345.42 | | - 345.16 | | | | |

## Choose your AEROBIC exercise!

### Exercise for today:

_____

**Day 6**

4-5 • © Summer Fit Activities™

 **Alliteration**

Alliteration is a figure of speech. Alliteration is the repetition of the same sounds or of the same kinds of sounds at the beginning of words or in stressed syllables.

**1. Read this example of alliteration by Mother Goose and copy it in your best handwriting below.**

Peter Piper picked a peck of pickled peppers.

A peck of pickled peppers Peter Piper picked.

If Peter Piper picked a peck of pickled peppers,

Where's the peck of pickled peppers Peter Piper picked?

_____

_____

_____

_____

2. Five freckled frogs frolicked freely in the forest.
The satiny snake slithered sideways across the slippery street.

**Make up your own alliteration and write it below.**

_____

_____

_____

_____

**Write the numbers in words.**

1. 428,754 _____

2. 7,402,567 _____

3. 9,567,428 _____

**Write in numbers.**

4. Six hundred thirteen thousand, three hundred nineteen. _____

5. Three million, five hundred sixty one thousand, six hundred six. _____

6. Ten million, eighty thousand, two hundred eighty seven. _____

7. The show starts at 7:15 p.m. and ends at 9:28 p.m.  How long is the movie?

   _____.

8. Chad starts football camp at 8:15.  If camp is 5 hours and 20 minutes long, what time

   will he be finished? _____

**Units of Measurement**

**Choose the best way to measure length of the item:  inches, feet, yards.**

| | | | |
|---|---|---|---|
| 9. bike = _____ | 11. hairbrush = _____ | 13. snake = _____ | 15. fence = _____ |
| 10. sailboat = _____ | 12. pencil  = _____ | 14. swimming pool = _____ | 16. field = _____ |

**Choose the best way  to measure weight: ounces, pounds, tons.**

| | | | |
|---|---|---|---|
| 17. hamburger = _____ | 19. bag of sugar = _____ | 21. truck = _____ | 23. basketball = _____ |
| 18. baseball = _____ | 20. elephant = _____ | 22. bike = _____ | 24. shoe = _____ |

## Choose your STRENGTH exercise!

**Day 7**

**Exercise for today:**

_____

Recored in
Fitness Log

4-5 • © Summer Fit Activities™

 **Alphabetical Order**

**Write each group of words in alphabetical order. Think of a title for the group that tells what the words best represent.**

1.   Utah,   Arizona,   New Mexico,   California,   Nevada

2.   Huron,   Michigan,   Superior,   Ontario,   Erie

3.   Fresno,   San Diego,   Bakersfield,   Long Beach,   Los Angeles

4.   hawk,   falcon,   eagle,   osprey,   vulture

5.   katydid,   dragonfly,   ladybug,   walking stick,   mosquito

| _____ | _____ | _____ | _____ | _____ |
|---|---|---|---|---|
| Group 1 | Group 2 | Group 3 | Group 4 | Group 5 |
| _____ | _____ | _____ | _____ | _____ |
| _____ | _____ | _____ | _____ | _____ |
| _____ | _____ | _____ | _____ | _____ |
| _____ | _____ | _____ | _____ | _____ |
| _____ | _____ | _____ | _____ | _____ |

**Look at these guide words from a dictionary page.  Divide each word into syllables and write it on the line. Write how many syllables it has.  Then write the words in alphabetical order.**

| Word | Number of syllables | Word | Number of syllables |
|---|---|---|---|
| 6. **Ex.** hazardous | haz  ar  dous   3 | 12. healthy | _____ |
| 7. headstrong | _____ | 13. hippopotamus | _____ |
| 8. haystack | _____ | 14. hindrance | _____ |
| 9. headquarters | _____ | 15. Hawaii | _____ |
| 10. havoc | _____ | 16. happen | _____ |
| 11. headache | _____ | 17. heartache | _____ |

1. Circle all the prime numbers.

| |
|---|
| 2 3 4 5 6 7 8 9 10 11 12 13 14 15 16 17 18 19 20 21 22 23 24 25 26 27 28 29 30 31 32 33 34 35 36 37 38 39 40 41 42 43 44 45 46 47 48 49 50 |

2. What is the only even prime number less than 50? _____

**Find the factors.  Circle the common factors, write the greatest common factor (GCF)**

3. 45: _____     90: _____     GCF = _____

4. 32: _____     64: _____     GCF = _____

5. 12: _____     36: _____     GCF = _____

6. 54: _____     72: _____     GCF = _____

**Round each decimal to the nearest whole number.**

| | | |
|---|---|---|
| 7. 2.5 = _____ | 10. 28.3 = _____ | 13. 912.8 = _____ |
| 8. 138.97 = _____ | 11. 436.23 = _____ | 14. 451.90 = _____ |
| 9. 9.2 = _____ | 12. 75.9 = _____ | 15. 509.92 = _____ |

**Place Value. How many tens in all?**

| | | |
|---|---|---|
| 16. 500 = _____ tens | 18. 700 = _____ tens | 20. 1,420 = _____ tens |
| 17. 2,800 = _____ tens | 19. 1,500 = _____ tens | 21. 5,340 = _____ tens |

**How many hundreds in all?**

| | | |
|---|---|---|
| 22. 5,400 = _____ hundreds | 24. 29,900 = _____ hundreds | 26. 7,800 = _____ hundreds |
| 23. 46,380 = _____ hundreds | 25. 112,700 = ____ hundreds | 27. 74,200 = _____ hundreds |

## Choose your AEROBIC exercise!

**Exercise for today:**

_____

Recored in
Fitness Log

**Day**
**8**

4-5 • © Summer Fit Activities™

**Friendly Letter**

Write a letter to your teacher for the new school year. Tell him/her about yourself; include your strengths and some of the things you would like to work on in the new year. Include something you hope to learn. Use the five parts of a friendly letter: heading (date), salutation (Dear_____,), body, closing (Your student,), and the signature (your name). Use good sentences, proper capitalization, punctuation, and your best handwriting!

**The cross country team runs after school every day of the week. The bar graph lists the distances run for the first week of May.**

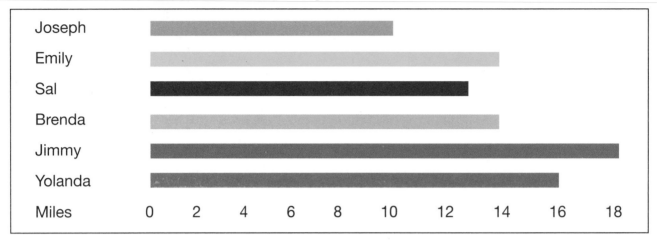

1. Who ran the fewest miles?_____

2. Who ran the most miles? _____

3. Which two runners ran the same number of miles? _____

4. How many miles did the team run in all for the week? _____

5. What is the average of all the miles run? _____

6. What is the median of all distances run? _____

7. Write Tally marks to represent the distance of each runner.

Joseph = _____     Emily = _____     Sal = _____

Brenda = _____     Jimmy = _____     Yolanda = _____

8. Write the distance run in Roman numerals.

Joseph = _____     Emily = _____     Sal = _____

Brenda = _____     Jimmy = _____     Yolanda = _____

**Choose your STRENGTH exercise!**

**Day 9**

**Exercise for today:**

_____

Recored in
Fitness Log

# FRIENDSHIP

Value

*Friendship is what comes from being friends. It is caring and being there for each other in good times and bad.*

**Lewis and Clark.** Meriwether Lewis and William Clark were explorers from the United States of America. They were friends over 200 years ago when the United States was still a new country and was made up of only 17 states. In 1803, U.S. President Thomas Jefferson asked Lewis and Clark to explore the unknown land beyond the Mississippi River. He asked them to discover and chart a passage to the west. Along the way, he wanted them to begin trading with the Native-American tribes, discover new plants and animals, and make maps and charts of it all so others could follow.

Together, Lewis and Clark went on an adventure of a lifetime. The two faced unknown dangers, obstacles, and hardships as they forged their way from the Mississippi River west to the Pacific Ocean. The journey took over two years and was very dangerous. Lewis and Clark knew the true value of friendship and cared about and respected each other. Through it all they stood by each other and showed teamwork, kindness, bravery, and loyalty.

**Count the number of syllables for each word from the story and write it.**

**1.** adventure _____

**2.** respected _____

**3.** Mississippi _____

**4.** dangerous _____

**5.** obstacles _____

**6.** tribes _____

**7.** discover _____

**8.** friendship _____

**9.** List three adventures you would like to have with a friend or family member.

_____

_____

_____

4-5 • © Summer Fit Activities™

# Value:

# FRIENDSHIP

"Don't walk behind me; I may not lead. Don't walk in front of me; I may not follow.  Just walk beside me and be my friend."

– Winnie the Pooh

```
H O N E S T W S Q M M H B E T O H L
P K K P K H U C V C Z S E R U D R U
G D X D O O C P P B H N U F E M S F
W A K W R Y R F I A G D V A Z D Q T
F U V E L O P D N J I V C A O S Y C
E G N M K L Y U O K L P E K W J R E
Y E L K K L I E H H O Q H H O O T P
G I J I K T D S U T Y Z Z C T M W S
E K N B A P Y K T J A M R D O Z B E
N D C U W T P X U E L L P W B G K R
Z R Y B W L M B K S N N R Q Z D B H
X R G G U F Q J S R P P S T K I M V
G W V C U K B D R Z W N N V G T A B
U P G J G K L D G X U T H B R I C I
Y I A F Q S X S U I B P R L L H E P
K N I P F B J Y D M R K U O J T Q P
```

**Find the words below that are qualities of a good friend.**

## WORD BANK

fun            listen

loyal          generous

honest         respectful

kind

## Be a Good Friend

 Invite a friend over.  Let them choose what to play first.

 Watch *Toy Story* with your family. Talk about how the characters in the movie portray true friendship.

 Make a friendship bracelet for one of your friends.  Give it to them and tell them why you are happy to be friends.

**Day 10**

## Choose a **Play** or **Exercise** Activity!

# Answer Pages

# Answer Key Grade 4-5

**P. 1-4**

**Summer Skills Review**

1. a. 2,654,000 b. 6,943,612
2. a. 500 b. 1,500 c. 6,800 d. 12,500
3. a. 5,000 b. 3,000
   c. 13,000 d. 28,000
4. a. 200,000 b. 600,000
   c. 600,000
5. a. 3/5   b. 11/20
   c. 25/100 or 1/4  d. 3 4/5
   e. 1 2/5
6. a. 11.92 b. 49,419 c. 8.06 d. 16,307
7. a. 7,145 b. 320 c. 275,132
8. 5,824 lbs.
9. a. 1,904 square cm. b. 45 ft.
10. 6,12,18,24,30,36,42,48,54,60.
11. 6: 1,2,3,6. 12: 1,2,3,4,6,12. GCF=6
12. figure drawn same size & shape.
13. 2 lines drawn to divide shape
    equally.
14. right angle drawn with 90
    degrees.
15. a. equilateral b. right c. acute
16. a. 28   b. 25   c. 19
17. 7,5,6,4,3,1.
18. Line drawn 3.5 inches.
19. a. 4/5 b. 6/12 or 1/2 c. 7/8 d. 4/15
20. a. I'm b. they're c. you're
    d. it's e. we'll f. he's
21. a. slowly b. awake c. boring
    d. dry (answers may vary.
22. a. intelligent b. thin c. glad
    d. sleepy (answers may vary.
23. a. pair b. flour
24. a. ? b. !,! c. .
25. a. Salt Lake CIty, Utah
    b. February 2, 1993
    c. 4:15 p.m. d. .
26. ran, played
27. favorite, baseball, new, red.
28. mouse, hole, wall.
29. me, her, we, it.
30. rain, ran, really, reject, rowing.
31. a. fish   b. mice   c. dogs
    d. men  e. ducks  f. foxes
32. a. water   b. flower
    c. write    d. button
33. a. Ave. b. Dr. c. in. d. Jan.
34. a. dis creet ly
35. a. ph b. ph c. gh d. lf e. gh
36. a. are b. was c. is d. were
37. a. ly b. est c. less d. ful
    (answers may vary.
38. My name is Elizabeth and I was
    born on January 30, 1999, in
    Omaha, Nebraska.
39. a. swam b. drew
    c. sang d. drank e. ran

**p. 7:**

1. B     2. D     3. D
4. Polaris, the North Star is one
   of the most well known stars
   because it always shines in the
   same position in the sky.

**p. 8:**

1. 50 2. 30 3. 100 4. 80 5. 150
6. 260 7. 280 8. 10 9. 540 10. 50
11. 5,000 12. 5 13. 50,000
14. 5 million 15. ten 16. 3
17. 4 18. 8 19. 20,000

**p. 9:**

1. can not    2. would not
3. they are  4. it is
5. have not  6. was not
7. did not    8. you are    9. she is
10. he is      11. are not
12. will not   13. they will
14. do not    15. has not  16. could not

**p. 10:**

1. 148        2. 38        3. 11,863
4. 10,034    5. 145.21    6. 344.56
7. 83         8. 664       9. 2,235
10. 48,143   11. 128.08   12. 107.19
13. 9         14. 9,000    15. 90
16. 90,000  17. 900      18. 900,000
19. 900 + 70 + 6
20. 9,000 + 800 + 60 + 5
21. 90,000 + 2,000 + 100 + 50 + 6

**p. 11:**

1. two        2. too        3. to, to
4. hour      5. our        6. through
7. threw    8. pair       9. pear
10. There   11. their     12. knew
13. new.

**p. 12:**

1. eight thousand seven hundred
   thirty-four
2. five hundred two thousand three
   hundred fifty-six
3. twelve thousand five hundred
   sixty-seven
4. sixty- seven thousand nine
   hundred two 5. 5,362
6. 10,971    7. 108,654   8. 2,115,621
9. 8,365     10. 15,498

**p. 13:** prey, excellent, talons, largest,
   eyes, night, bald, clean, dead.

**p. 14:**

1. 400        2. 700        3. 800
4. 400        5. 300        6. 800
7. 300        8. 200        9. 200
10. 5,000    11. 2,000    12. 1,000
13. 6,000    14. 4,000    15. 3,000
16. 8,000    17. 6,000    18. 2,000
19. 60,000  20. 120,000
21. 80,000  22. 470,000

**p. 15:**

1. slavery     2. Honest Abe
3. president
4. trusted 5. answers vary

**p. 19:**

1. Ave.        2. Dr.        3. Mr.
4. St.          5. tsp.        6. lb.
7. oz =ounce, cm. = centimeter,
   doz. = dozen, ft. = feet, qt. =
   quart, yd. = yard, wk. = week.

**p. 20:**

1. 1/2        2. 3/5        3. 1/6
4. 1/2        5. 1/2        6. 1/4
7. 1/3        8. 1/3        9. 1/4
10. 2/4      11. 10/30    12. 2/8
13. 0.6      14. .05        15. .03
16. .5        17. .04        18. .01
19. .8        20. .07        21. .3

Correct work every day or two to help keep students accountable. This also shows your child you are interested in their worK

# Answer Key Grade 4-5

**p. 21:**
2. insects, spider crossed off
3. fruits, carrot crossed off
4. states, China crossed off
5. colors, two crossed off
6. tastes, sugar crossed off.

**p. 22:**
1. 812  2. 697  3. 6,046  4. 10,497
5. 1,064     6. 6,085     7. 37,945
8. 54,656  9. 754     10. 4,376
11. 65,168  12. 336,979
13. circled numbers:
    17,21,111,267,521,1,987.

**p. 23:**
1. least important person on the team.
2. right away
3. raining heavily
4. a small amount of money
5. running out of time
6. don't talk back no matter what
7-10. answers vary.

**p. 24:**
2. 3 $1, 1 quarter, 3 pennies.
3. 1 $5, 2 $1, 2 quarters, 1 nickel,
    1 penny.
4. 1 $5, 4 $1, 3 quarters, 1 dime,
    4 pennies.
5. 2 $5, 2 quarters, 2 dimes,
    2 pennies.
6. 4 $1, 3 quarters.
7. 1 $5, 1 $1, 1 quarter, 2 dimes,
    4 pennies.
8. $18.63

**p. 25:**
1. three
2. nerves, messages
3. cerebrum
4. senses, speech     5. cerebellum
6. brain stem     7. spinal cord
8. nerves, messages, parts,
    things, halves, hemispheres,
    movements, senses, thoughts,
    muscles, movements, eyes, ears.

**p. 26:**
1. 1,617  2. 11,945  3. 74,936  4. 17,442
5. 5,384     6. 18,360     7. 49,889
8. 16,740  9. 1,480     10. 56,151
11. 27,060  12. 59,256  13. 3,588
14. 17,750  15. 11,750  16. 26,196
17. 48,60,72,84,96,108,120,132,144.

**p. 27:**
1. poor, sick, dying, lonely
2. generosity, kindness, love
3. India.

**p. 31:**
1. an     2. a     3. an
4. a     5. an     6. an
7. a     8. an     9. a
10. an     11. this     12. these
13. this     14. these     15. this
16. these     17. this     18. these
19. these

**p. 32:**  22 cm, 72 in, 140 m, 9 , 15.

**p. 33:**
1. sings     2. barked     3. baked
4. blew     5. dribbled  6. played
7. read, checked.
(8-13 answers vary. 8. built
9. rode     10. played     11. slithered
12. shrieked 13. ate

**p. 34:**
1. 35%
2. 5 (birds, dogs, fish, cats, lizards.
3. lizard 4. 10%  5. dog     6. 28%

**p. 35:**
1. lions     2. peaches  3. wolves
4. pennies  5. leaves     6. cakes
7. feet     8. mice     9. beliefs
10. girls     11. scarves  12. babies
13. thieves  14. deer     15. men
16. benches 17. dogs     18. classes
19. cats     20. toes     21. boys
22. nouns.

**p. 36:**
1. <     2. =     3. <
4. =     5. <     6. <
7. =     8. >     9. =
10. <     11. >     12. =
13. <     14. <     15. >
16. 604.8  17. 170.7     18. 383.2
19. 660.6

**p. 37:**
1. your 2. their 3. It's 4. meet 5. he'll
6. Our, they're  7. Who's   8. You're
9. its     10. new     11. I'll, aisle
12. where  13. threw     14. bear
15. weak, its.

**p. 38:** plot points, answers vary.

**p. 39:** answers vary

**p. 43:**
1. . imperative     2. ? interrogative
3. . declarative
4. . declarative     5. . imperative
6. ! exclamatory
7. ? interrogative
8. ! ! exclamatory. 9. answers vary.

**p. 44:**
1. 95.96 2. 161.06 3. 43.01  4. 316.35
5. 255.98     6. 102.16     7. 79.20
8. 112.61     9. 445.1     10. 1497.73
11. 102.22     12. 87.08     13. 63.7

**p. 45:**
1. newer     2. noisier
3. most delicious  4. faster
5. funniest  6. most fascinating
7. slowest  8. sweeter
9. most difficult     10. warmest

**p. 46:**
1. 2     2. 4     3. 3
4. 15     5. 6     6. 2
7. 6     8. 4     9. 12
10. 9     11. 6     12. 8
13. 52, 529, 5295, 15,295, 52,956,
    515,295.
14. 186, 268, 2,687, 27,687, 28,675,
    268,187.

Reward well
done and
completed work
with stickers,
stamps or
hand written
messages

# Answer Key

**p. 47:**
1. head + ache
2. every + where
3. life + guard
4. second + hand
5. home + less
6. birth + day
7. snake + skin
8. basket + ball

**p. 48:**
1. 830 lbs.
2. $35.24
3. 5 slices
4. 79 degrees
5. 48 hours
6. 6 hours

**p. 49:**
1. chose
2. wrote
3. threw
4. ran
5. knew
6. made
7. rode
8. grew
9. sang
10. felt
11. slept
12. hid
13. sold
14. heard
15-18. answers vary

**p. 50:**
1. 5
2. 2
3. 7
4. 7
5. 7
6. 3
7. 6
8. 9
9. 6
10. 8
11. 9
12. 8
13. 10
14. 4
15. 8
16. 9
17. 78 r. 3
18. 491
19. 144
20. 857
21. 356
22. 672
23. 742
24. 921

**P. 51:** answers vary

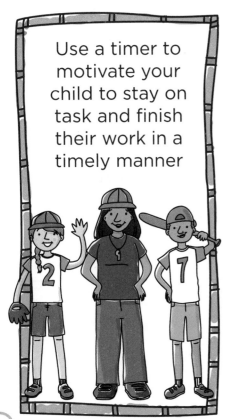

Use a timer to motivate your child to stay on task and finish their work in a timely manner

**p. 55:**
1. crust
2. outer core
3. inner core
4. mantle

**p. 56:**
1. 16,912
2. 2,688
3. 8,850
4. 350
5. 1,400

**p. 57:**
1. laughed
2. unfairly
3. deliberately
4. disorder
5. creepy
6. buy
7. late

**p. 58:**
1. right
2. obtuse
3. acute
4. acute
5. right
6. octagon, ,8,0

**p. 59:**
1. false
2. true
3. true
4. false
5. true
6. true
7. captivating and very interesting.

**p. 60:**
1. 611
2. 54.19
3. 368
4. 34.17
5. 429
6. 52.89
7. 151
8. 12.80
9. 18
10. 2.9
11. 966 square in.
12. 4,410 square ft.
13. 22 R.1
14. 17 R. 2
15. 14 R. 3
16. 20 R. 3
17. 13 R1

**p. 61:**
1-8: answers vary
9. store
10. girl
11. team
12. lake
13. holiday
14. country
15. car
16. dog
17. France circled, summer underlined
18. Despicable Me circled, movie underlined
19. Liberty Park and Memorial Day circled, picnic underlined
20. Twinkle...and Maddie circled, sister underlined.
21. Jacob, Pedro, Elm Street, Maple Avenue circled, friends and corner underlined.
22. January and Columbus, Ohio circled 23. Basset Hound and December circled, puppies underlined.
24. Mrs. Smith, Mr. Dean, Lincoln Heights circled, librarian, school, and librarian underlined.

**p. 62:**
1. 4/10=2/5
2. 7/8
3. 6/8 = 3/4
4. 14/21 = 2/3
5. 5/6
6. 5/12
7. 3/16
8. 9/12=3/4
9. 4/20 = 1/5
10. 7/9
11. 7/8
12. 5/20 = 1/4
13. 1/10
14. 1/5
15. 1/6
16. 1/4
17. 1/2
18. 6/7
19. 2/5
20. 1/9
21. 1/5

**p. 63:**
1. visited adults and children, helped sick, poor and lonely.
2. extraordinary.
3. nice

**p. 67:**
1. passed, past
2. really
3. about
4. again
5. sometimes
6. doesn't
7. Their
8. They're
9. there
10. write
11. right
12. our, well. meet
13. who's
14. are
15. good

**p. 68:**
1. 30
2. 168
3. 5
4. 12
5. 12
6. 300
1. 5
2. 4
3. 84
1. 5
2. 10
3. 20
4. 45
1. 9
2. 53
3. 90
4. 22

**p. 69:**
1. Baton Rouge
2. Georgia, Virginia
3. Helen Keller
4. Kansas
5. Arizona
6. Virginia
7. Montgomery
8. Alabama, Arizona, Georgia, Kansas, Louisiana, Virginia.
9. Jan. 2, 1788
10. Geronimo, Arizona.

**p. 70:**
1. 1, 2,3,4,5,6,
2. 2,4,6,8,10,12
3. 3,6,9,12,15,18
4. 8,16,24,40,48,56,64,72,80,88
5. 5,15,20,25,40,45,55,60,75,90,100
6. 3,6,9,12,15,18; 5,10,15,20,25; LCM=15
7. 45
8. 88
9. 10,20,30,40,50,60,70,80,90,100

**p. 71:**
1. adjective
2. adverb
3. adjective
4. adverb
5. adjective
6. adverb
7. adverb
8. adjective
9. adverb
10. adverb
11. bigger biggest
12. smaller, smallest

4-5 • © Summer Fit Activities"

# Answer Key

13. sadder, saddest
14. sleepier, sleepiest
15. more interesting, most interesting
16. shorter, shortest
17. more useful, most useful
18. happier, happiest.

**p. 72:**
1. 1,3,6
2. 1,2,3,4,6,12
3. 1,5,25
4. 1,2,5,10
5. 1,2,3,6,9,18
6. 1,2,4,8,16
7. 1,2,4,8,16; 1,2,3,4,6,8,12,24 GCF= 8
8. 1,3,5,15; 1,2,3,5,6,10,15,30; GCF=15
9. 3 hours 10 minutes
10. 4:00 pm
11. 9:15 am

**p. 73:**
1. a
2. c
3. a
4. d
5. b

**p. 74:**
1. 21
2. 24
3. 3
4. 36
5. 16
6. 2
7. 3
8. 108
9. 360
10. 168
11. 8
12. 2
13. 3.4,3.7
14. 30,60,90
15. 4 1/2, 4 3/4, 5, 5 1/2, 5 3/4
16. 6,2,10,40,3; Divide by 8

**p. 75:**
Circled answers: standing up for someone who is being bullied, admitting your mistake, helping others, walking away from a fight, doing what is right, working hard and trying again.

**p. 79:**
1. thing, thing, place, person, person.
2. thing, place, person, thing, thing.
3. place, person, place, place, person.
4. zoo
5. boy
6. water park
7. grandma
8. girl
9. pilot
10. rattle snake
11. my
12. mine
13. your
14. our
15. his
16. her
17. hers
18. your
19. their.

**p. 80:**
1. 18
2. 6
3. 17
4. 75
5. 16
6. 14
7. 8
8. 30
9. $3.00
10. $49.00
11. $13.00
12. $52.00
13. $118.00
14. $287.00
15. $99.00
16. $105.00
17. $26.00
18. $244.00
19-22. answers vary but should have 2 division & 2 multiplication equations

**p. 81:**
1. semiyearly= twice a year
2. rewrite= write again
3. preorder = order before
4. midfield= middle of the field
5. unclear = not clear
6. supersize= large size
7. impossible = not possible
8. irregular = not regular
9. bicycle= cycle with 2 wheels
10. submerge= put below.

**p. 82:**
1. 700
2. 500
3. 4,400
4. 12,300
5. 1,200
6. 300
7. 4,600
8. 1,300
9. 500
10. 7,000
11. 6,000
12. 7,000
13. 2,000
14. 16,000
15. 23,000
16. 8,000
17. 113,000
18. 3,000
19. 30,000
20. 50,000
21. 140,000
22. 60,000
23. 80,000
24. 270,000
25. 20,000
26. 10,000
27. 530,000
1. 245,252,1,254, 2,450, 21,652.
2. 595, 5,095, 10,500, 15,657, 51,501.
3. 19,799, 99,198, 909,000, 919,001, 999,023.

**p. 83:**
1-6. words vary, examples:
1. unfriendly,friendless, friendship, friendly
2. unfaithful, faithfully faithful, unfaithfully
3. incorrect, corrected, incorrectly, correctly
4. completed, completely, completion,
5. cooking, cooked, cooker, uncooked
6. react, reaction, action, acting, reacted.
7. kind
8. navigate
9. courage
10. celebrate
11. complete
12. weak
13. legislate
14. shy
15. fruit
16. announce

**p. 84:**
1. parallel
2. intersecting
3. perpendicular
4. *----------------------------
5 *----------------------*
6. parallelogram, 4 7. pentagon, 5,0.

**p. 85:** Answers vary
ex: 1. the cupcakes burned.

**p. 86:**
1. 10,15,20,12,18,24,14,21,28.
2. 6,10,16,21,35,56,0,0,0,18,30,48,12, 20,32
3. 21,24,27,42,48,54,49,56,63,56,64,7 2,63,72,81
4. 4:40
5. 1,265,429
6. 2,347,083
7. 573,652

**p. 87:**
1. India
2. valuable, respect
3. yourself
4. peacefully
5. answers vary

**p. 91:** answers vary

**p. 92:**
1. 1/12
2. 1/6
3. A= 3,6 B=5,9 C=7,6 D=3,3 E=9,4

**p. 93:**
1. make dough
2. roll out and put on baking sheet
3. sauce
4. cheese and topping
5. bakes
6. cut and eat
7. answers vary

Have your child correct their own work while you read off the answers. This will reinforce the skills they just practiced

# Answer Key

**p. 94:**
1. 1/3        2. 2/5        3. 1/2
4. 4 1/2      5. 7          6. 4 1/2
7. pictures vary
1. .25        2. .13        3. .5
4. .50        5. .7         6. .8
7. .85        8. .33        9. 1 1/2
10. 1 1/2     11. 1/2       12. 2/3
13. 2/8, 2/7, 4/8, 2/3
14. =         15. =         16. >
17. >         18. <         19. =
20. =         21. >         22. >

**p. 95:**
1. F          2. S          3. F
4. S          5. S          6. F
7. S          8. F
9. We watered our garden and the plants grew quickly.
10. Anne goes to ballet every Saturday but Joy goes on Monday.
11. Michael took his canoe to the lake so he could go fishing.
12. Noah could choose chocolate or vanilla ice cream.

**p. 96:**
1. acute      2. straight   3. right
4. obtuse     5. acute      6. obtuse
7. right      8. obtuse     9. acute

**p. 97:**
2. air        3. vegetable
4. day        5. year       6. out
7. sad        8. light      9. puppy
10. sky       11. foot      12. baseball
13. cold      14. summer
15-16. answers vary

**p. 98:**
1. congruent
2. not congruent
3. congruent
4. not congruent
5. not congruent
6. congruent
7-9. answers vary

**p. 99:**  6, 7, 1, 3, 2, 5, 4.

**p. 103:**
1. wide       2. gushed     3. happy
4. incomplete  5. worthless
6. slowly     7. reject     8. gentle
9. visible    10. reality   11. land
12. gentle    13. sink      14. lengthy
15. harmful

**p. 104:** Shapes divided symmetrically.
11. Q          12. BALD

**p. 105:**
1. Atlantic Ocean
2. navigator , Canada, mystery
3. doomed              4. answers vary.

**p. 106:**
1. 5 2. 100 3. 10 4. 100 5. 5 6. 36
7. century 8. weeks, month 9. years 10. days
11. 4 12. 18 13. 21,120 14. 6 15. 2 16. 54
17. 49,28,8,2 18. 600, 1 ,2, 1,440.

**p. 107:** answers vary

**p. 108:**
1. 560 2. 620 3. 980 4. 1,580
5. 2,460 6. 1,140 7. 2,790 8. 5,370
9. 4,350 10. 5 11. 7 12. 10 13. 12
14. 41 15. 78 16. 8.5 17. 97
18. 23 19. 28 20. x 21. 356
22. 630 23. 10 24. 572 25. 930
26. 402 27. 20,30,50,100, 90
28. 30

**p. 109:** answers vary

**p. 110:**
1. 64          2. 180        3. 48
4. 108         5. 2 cubic feet

**p. 111:**
1. overcome fear
2. Learn to swim and surf with one arm
3. answers vary

**p. 115:**
1. H 2. M 3. P 4. S 5. H 6. P 7. S 8. M
9. P 10. M 11. S

**p. 116:**
1. $9.00 2. $15.00 3. $28.00 4. $3.00
5. $30.00 6. $50.00 7. $10.00
8. $70.00 9. $400.00 10. $400.00
11. $700.00 12. $400.00 13. $70.00
14. $30.00 15. $100.00 16. $800.00
17. $180,741 18. 806.29 19. 333.04
20. 1.134 21. 3.24

**p. 117:** answers vary

**p. 118:**
1. four hundred twenty-eight thousand seven hundred fifty-four
2. seven million four hundred two thousand five hundred sixty-seven
3. nine million five hundred sixty-seven thousand four hundred twenty-eight
4. 613,319    5. 3,561,606
6. 10,080,287  7. 2 hours 13 minutes
8. 1:35        9. ft.         10. yd.,ft.
11. in.        12. in.        13. in.
14. yd.,ft.    15. ft.        16. yd.
17. oz.        18. oz         19. lb
20. ton        21. ton        22. lbs.
23. oz.        24. oz.

**p. 119:**
1. States: Arizona, California, Nevada, New Mexico, Utah
2. Lakes : Erie, Huron, Michigan, Ontario, Superior
3. Cities: Bakersfield, Fresno, Long Beach, Los Angeles, San Diego
4. Birds of prey: eagle, falcon, hawk, osprey, vulture
5. insects: dragonfly, katydid, ladybug, mosquito, walking stick
6. haz ar dous 3 7. head strong 2
8. hay stack 2        9. head quarters 3
10. hav oc 2          11. headache 2
12. heal thy 2 13. hip po po to mus 5
14. hin drance 2         15. Haw ai i 3
16. hap pen 2         17. heart ache 2

**p. 120:**
1. 2,3,5,7,11,13,17,19,23,29,31,37,41,43,47
2. 2
3. 1,3,5,9,15,45; ,2,3,6,9,10,15,30,45,90 GCF = 45
4. 1,2,4,8,16,32; 1,2,4,8,16,32,64 GCF= 32
5. 1,2,3,4,6,12; 1,2,3,4,6,12,18,36 GCF=12
6. 1,2,3,6,9,18,27,54; ,2,3,4,6,12,18,24,36,72 GCF: 18
7. 3   8. 139   9. 9   10. 28   11. 436
12. 76   13. 913   14. 452   15. 510
16. 50   17. 280   18. 70   19. 150
20. 142   21. 534   22. 54   23. 463.8
24. 299   25. 1,127   26. 78   27. 742

**p. 121:** answers vary

**p. 122:**
1. Joseph 2. Jimmy 3. Emily, Brenda
4. 84 miles   5. 12 6. 14 7. Tally marks
8. Joseph X , Emily XIV, Sal XII, Brenda XIV, Jimmy XVIII, Yolanda XVI.

**p. 123:**
3,3,4,3,3,1,3,2

# Summer Fit Book Report I

Title: _____

Author: _____

Illustrator: _____

Setting (Where the story takes place): _____

Main Character(s):

_____

_____

_____

Write your favorite part of the story
(use separate sheet of paper if needed):

_____

_____

_____

_____

_____

_____

_____

_____

_____

_____

Tell your favorite part of the story to a parent, guardian or friend.

Read a variety of books on topics that interest you already and new areas that you want to explore!

131

# Summer Fit Book Report II

Title: _____

Author: _____

Illustrator: _____

Setting (Where the story takes place): _____

Main Character(s):

_____

_____

_____

Write your favorite part of the story
(use separate sheet of paper if needed):

_____

_____

_____

_____

_____

_____

_____

_____

_____

_____

_____

Tell your favorite part of the story to a parent, guardian or friend.

Read a variety of books on topics that interest you already and new areas that you want to explore!

# Summer Fit Book Report III

Title: _____

Author: _____

Illustrator: _____

Setting (Where the story takes place): _____

Main Character(s):

_____

_____

_____

Write your favorite part of the story
(use separate sheet of paper if needed):

_____

_____

_____

_____

_____

_____

_____

_____

_____

_____

Tell your favorite part of the story to a parent, guardian or friend.

Read a variety of books on topics that interest you already and new areas that you want to explore!

# Summer Fit Book Report IV

Title: _____

Author: _____

Illustrator: _____

Setting (Where the story takes place): _____

Main Character(s):

_____

_____

_____

Write your favorite part of the story
(use separate sheet of paper if needed):

_____

_____

_____

_____

_____

_____

_____

_____

_____

Tell your favorite part of the story to a parent, guardian or friend.

Read a variety of books
on topics that interest you
already and new areas that
you want to explore!

# HEALTH
# &
# NUTRITION

4-5 • © Summer Fit Activities™

# Let's Play

## There are so many ways to play! Check off the different activities as you play them, have fun!"

Everybody has different abilities and interests, so take the time to figure out what activities and exercises you like. Try them all: soccer, dance, karate, basketball, and skating are only a few. After you have played a lot of different ones, go back and focus on the ones you like!

Create your own ways to be active and combine different activities and sports to put your own twist on things. Talk with your parents or caregiver for ideas and have them help you find and do the activities that you like to do. Playing and exercising is a great way to help you become fit, but remember that the most important thing about playing is that you are having fun!

# List of Exercise Activities

## Home–Outdoor:

Walking
Ride Bicycle
Swimming
Walk Dog
Golf with whiffle balls outside
Neighborhood walks/Exploring
(in a safe area)
Hula Hooping
Rollerskating/Rollerblading
Skateboarding
Jump rope
Climbing trees
Play in the back yard
Hopscotch
Stretching
Basketball
Yard work
Housecleaning

## Home – Indoor:

Dancing
Exercise DVD
Yoga DVD
Home gym equipment
Stretch bands
Free weights
Stretching

## With friends or family:

Red Rover
Chinese jump rope
Regular jump rope
Ring around the rosie
Tag/Freeze
Four score
Capture the flag
Dodgeball
Slip n Slide
Wallball
Tug of War
Stretching
Run through a sprinkler
Skipping
Family swim time
Bowling
Basketball
Hiking
Red light, Green light
Kick ball
Four Square
Tennis
Frisbee
Soccer
Jump Rope
Baseball

**Turn off TV Go Outside - PLAY!**
Public Service Announcement
Brought to you by Summer Fit

## Chill out on Screen Time

Screen time is the amount of time spent watching TV, DVDs or going to the movies, playing video games, texting on the phone and using the computer. The more time you spend looking at a screen the less time you are outside riding your bike, walking, swimming or playing soccer with your friends. Try to spend no more than a couple hours a day in front of a screen for activities other than homework and get outside and play!

4-5 • © Summer Fit Activities"

# HEALTHY BODIES

There are many ways to enrich your life by eating healthy, exercising each day and playing! Keeping your body strong and healthy will help you feel good and even perform better in school. To be healthy, you need to eat right, get enough sleep and exercise. What you learn and do with Summer Fit Activities™ is just the beginning. From here, you will be able to find other healthy and active things to do based on your interests, abilities and personal goals.

 Aerobic Exercises help your cardiovascular system that includes your heart and blood vessels. You need a strong heart to pump blood. Your blood delivers oxygen and nutrients to your body.

 Strength Exercises help you make your muscles stronger and increase your muscular endurance. Endurance helps you get the most from your muscles before you get tired!

 Flexibility Exercises are good for many reasons including warming up before you do aerobic or strength exercises. Flexibility also helps you use all your muscles in different ways, positions and ranges of motion.

Your body composition is made up of lean mass and fat mass. Lean mass includes water, muscles and organs in your body. Fat mass includes fat your body needs for later and stores for energy.

Exercise helps you burn body fat and do more of the activities you want to do like hiking, biking and playing at the beach. There are a lot fun sports and activities to choose from that will help you strengthen your body and your brain!

## Get Active!

| Apple | Brain |
|-------|-------|
| Water | Vegetable |
| Exercise | Muscles |
| Aerobic | Organs |
| Strength | Fun |
| Flexibility | Play |

```
D G L H B J S Z V Z B R F P C
Y H V T T E V E V A Z Y L F I
A C U P L G G M Y K I V E S B
G O T C A E N G H T P W X M O
H E S X T L M E Y A L P I L R
A U Y A E S I C R E X E B V E
M P B Y B M R G B T H Z I Q A
I L P R O L S V V F S R L K X
E Y A L D P E N B G A R I I I
F I B P E L H Y U V I F T W N
N G T D J A U D L F Z Q Y A X
O N M C X A V R S I V J S T J
O R G A N S B W A K K R A E C
J T C E L Y R C U Z R B G R P
X J P Y A W W E O S C K I K J
```

# Active Lifestyle Pop Quiz!

## What does being active mean to you?

List your 3 favorite aerobic activities

1) _____

2) _____

3) _____

EX:

*bicycling, running, swimming, skateboarding, hiking*

List 2 sports you like to play

1) _____

2) _____

EX:

*lacrosse, basketball, baseball, dance, volleyball*

List 3 activities you like that help build strength and flexibility:

1) _____

2) _____

3) _____

EX:

*yoga, dance, gymnastics, martial arts, jump rope*

List 3 fun things you like to do that get you moving

1) _____

2) _____

3) _____

EX:

*bowling, skating, fishing, gardening, cooking*

List 2 things you can limit that will help you be more active:

1) _____

2) _____

EX:

*video games, TV, phone*

List 3 things you can do to help the environment and get you moving more often!

1) _____

2) _____

3) _____

EX:

*pick up trash in neighborhood, separate items in recycling bins, help plant a garden, wash your water cup and reuse, ride your bike*

4-5 • © Summer Fit Activities™

# Summer Fitness Program

The goal of your Summer Fitness program is to help you improve in all areas of physical fitness and to be active every day.

You build cardiovascular endurance through aerobic exercise. For aerobic exercise, you need to work large muscle groups that get your heart pumping and oxygen moving through your entire body. This increases your heart rate and breathing.  On your aerobic day, you can jog, swim, hike, dance, skateboard, ride your bike, roller blade... there are so many to choose from!

Your goal should be to try to get 30 minutes a day of aerobic exercise at least 2-3 times a week. Follow your daily Summer Fit™ exercise schedule and choose your own aerobic exercises along the way.

You build your muscular strength and muscle endurance with exercises that work your muscles, like push-ups, sit-ups and pull-ups. Increase how many you can do of each of these over time and pay attention to your Summer Fit™ daily exercises for other activities that help build strong muscles.

Get loose – stretch. Warming up before you exercise if very important. It prepares your body for exercising by loosening your muscles and getting your body ready for training. An easy start is to shake your arms and roll your shoulders!

# Time to Hydrate

It is important to drink water before and after you exercise because water regulates your body temperature and gives you nutrients to keep you healthy.

The next time you exercise, drink a cup of water before and after you are done.

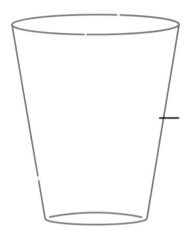

Color the bottom half of the cup red below to represent the water you drink before you exercise. Color the top half of the cup blue to represent the water you drink after you exercise.

# Water Facts

There is the same amount of water on earth today as there was when dinosaurs roamed through our backyards!

75% of your brain is water!

Water regulates the earth's temperature.

Water is made up of two elements, hydrogen and oxygen. Its chemical formula is $H_2O$

Water is essential for life on earth.

Here are instructions for your daily exercises. Talk with a parent about setting goals. Set your goals for time or reps. Keep track of your goals using your Summer Fitness Chart. Have fun!

# Aerobic Exercises and Activities

**Jogging in Place:** Run slowly in place or outside to accomplish your time goal.

**Bump and Jump:** Jump forward and back, jump side to side. Hop on one foot to another, moving side-to-side, alternating feet. Quicken your pace.

**Let's Dance:** Step to your right with your right foot (putting your weight on your right foot). Step behind your right foot with your left foot (putting your weight on your left foot). Step again to the right with your right foot (weight on right) and touch your left foot next to your right (with your weight staying on the right foot). Repeat the above going left but switching to the other foot.
Goal = Dance for 5 minutes
Do the Cha-cha  Step forward right, cha-cha Step forward left, cha-cha Repeat
Do the Cross over  Cross right over left, kick out right leg then backwards cha-cha-cha Cross left over right, kick out left leg then backwards cha-cha-cha  Repeat
Do the Rope  Rope 1/4 to the left 1/4 facing the rear 1/4 turn left again Rope to the front and step together with a clap. Repeat  (When you "rope" hold one hand above your head and swing your arms in a circle like you have a rope above you).

**Pass and Go:** This activity requires a second person. Ask a friend or someone from your family to play with you. The object of this activity is to pass a ball back and forth counting by 2's get to a 100 as fast as you can. Have a stopwatch handy. Set a time you want to beat and go! Increase your goal by setting a lower time. Repeat.

**Step It Up:** This activity uses stairs if you have them. If you do, take three trips up and down the stairs. Raise your legs high like you are in a marching band. If you do not have stairs, do 20 step-ups on one step. Start slow and increase your speed.

**Kangaroo Bounce:** Tape a shoelace to the floor in a straight line. Stand on one side of the string with both feet together. Jump forward over the string and then backward to land in your original place. Take a short break—and do it again. This time jump side-to-side over the shoelace.

**Garbage Hoops:** A trashcan makes a great indoor basketball goal— perfect for a quick game of one-on-one against yourself or a friend! Use a bottle-cap or crunched up ball of paper as your basketball. Twist, jump and make sure to use a few fakes to win the game! First one to 11 wins!

4-5 • © Summer Fit Activities™

**Green Giant:** Mow the grass, weed the garden or pick up your yard. Feeling good today? Mow your neighbors yard too!

**Capture the Flag:** Use scarves or old T-shirts for flags. Assign a different color one for each team. Use chalk, cones, tape, or landmarks such as trees or sidewalks to divide your playing area into equal-sized territories for each team. Place one flag into each territory. It must be visible and once it is placed it cannot be moved. When the game begins, players cross into opposing teams' territories to grab their flags. When a player is in an opposing team's territory they can be captured by the other team. Once they are tagged he/she must run to the sideline and perform an exercise—for example, five jumping jacks or three push-ups. After they perform their exercise the player can go back to their team territory and resume play. The game ends when one team successfully captures the flag(s) from the other team or teams and returns to their own territory with the opposing team's flag.

**Happy Feet:** Use your feet every chance you get today. Walk to a friend's house, to the store, around the park or wherever it's safe to walk. Get your parents to walk with you after dinner.

**Let's Roll:** Put your lungs to work on your bike, skates or scooter. Don't forget to wear helmets and pads!

**Speed:** Walk a block, than run as fast as you can the next block. Alternate between walking and running blocks. Rest in between. Time yourself and see if you can beat your original time. Repeat. Goal = 2 blocks

**Tag:** Decide who is "IT." Choose the boundaries for the game. If a player crosses the boundaries during the game, he/she is automatically "IT."
Give players a 15 second head start. "IT" counts to 15 and then chases the others to tag them! The player who has been tagged is now "IT!"

**Hide and Seek:** Select an area to play. Designate a specific area with clear boundaries. Have everyone gather around a tree or other landmark, which is "home base." Whoever goes first must close his/her eyes and count to 10. Everybody else hides during the count. After the count is over, call out "Ready or not here I come!" Now it's time to look for the other players who are hiding. They are trying to get to home base before they are found. If they get to home base without being found they are "safe." The first player found loses and they start the next game by counting to 10!

**Hula-Hoop:** Hold the hula-hoop around your waist with both hands. Pull it forward so it is resting against your back. With both hands, fling the hoop to the left so that rolls in a circle around your body. Do this a few times until you get the feel of it. Leave the hula-hoop on the ground for a few minutes and practice swirling your hip. Move your pelvis left, back, right, forward. Find a groove and keep the hoop going around your hips as long as you can. When it falls to the ground pick it up and try again!

**Jump Rope:** Start by holding an end of the rope in each hand. Position the rope behind you on the ground. Raise your arms up and turn the rope over your head bringing it down in front of you. When it reaches the ground, jump over it. Find a good pace, not too slow and not too fast. Jump over the rope each time it comes around. Continue until you reach your goal of jumping a certain amount of times without stopping.

4-5 • © Summer Fit Activities"

# Strength Exercises and Activities

**Knee lifts:** Stand with your feet flat on the floor. Start by lifting your right knee up 5 times, always bring both feet together between each interval then change legs. When you feel more confident, bounce while you bring your knee up and alternate between legs.

**Pushups:** Start in an elevated position. Keep your body straight, head facing forward. Lower yourself down by bending your elbows. Once your chest touches the ground, push back up to your starting position.

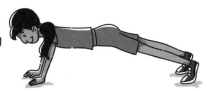

**Curl-ups:** Start by lying on the floor, knees bent and arms crossed in front. Rise up and forward until your chest touches your raised knee. As soon as you touch your knee, go back down slowly to your starting position.

**Squats:** Stand up straight with your legs shoulder width apart. Keep your ankles and legs pointed straight forward. Raise your arms in front of you during the exercise. Bend your knees and lower yourself down like you are going to sit in a chair until your bottom is in a straight line with your knees while keeping your back straight. If you cannot make it down this far, go as far as you can, hold for two seconds and slowly raise back up to your starting position.

**Chop n Squat:** Start with legs wide, bring your feet together, then out wide again, reach down and touch the ground, and pop up.

**Chin Ups:** Start by hanging from the bar with your arms fully extended, keeping your feet off the ground. Your hands should be facing into the bar with your palms on the bar itself. Pull yourself up until your chin touches the bar. When you touch the bar with your chin, slowly let yourself down to your starting position and repeat the exercise.

**Leg Raise:** Lie on your back with your legs straight in the air forming a 90- degree angle. Lower your legs downward, stopping a few inches from the ground. Pause, and return to your starting position. Keep your back flat on the floor the entire time.

**Balance:** Balance on one foot. Foot extended low in front of you. Foot extended low in back of you. Foot extended low to the side.

**Jumping Jacks:** Jump to a position with your legs spread wide and your hands touching overhead and then returning to a position with your feet together and arms at your sides. A more intense version is to bend down (over) and touch the floor in between each jump.

**Shoulder Rolls:** Place your arms at your side while standing at attention. Lift your shoulders into an "up" position and roll them forward while pulling into your chest.

**Lunges:** Stand straight with your legs shoulder width apart. Keep your hands at your side. Step forward with one leg, bending at your knee to lower your body. Move back into your starting position and repeat. Alternate between legs after performing a number of reps.

**Heel Raises:** Stand on the floor with your feet pointing forward and about one foot apart. Keep your knees straight, but do not lock them into place. Raise yourself up onto the balls of your feet and squeeze your calf muscle. Hold this position before releasing back into your starting position.

**Chair Dips:** Sit in a chair with your hands placed firmly on the arms of the chair. Extend your legs out so they are resting on your heels. Lift your bottom up from the chair by extending your arms straight up. Lower yourself down by bending your elbows into a 90-degree angle. Do not let your bottom touch the chair. Push back up and repeat the exercise.

**Crisscross:** Lie on your back with your shoulders 3-5 inches off the ground and your heels raised off the floor. Keep your mid and lower sections of your back flat on the floor and keep your abdominal muscles tight. Rest your arms next to you on the floor. Cross your left foot over the right foot. Without stopping, rotate your feet so the right is over your left foot. Continue this pattern without resting.

**Scissors:** Lie on your back with your shoulders 3-5 inches off the ground and your heels raised off the floor. Raise your legs 3-5 more inches higher while keeping your legs straight. Alternate between legs so you are creating a scissor motion with your legs going up and down opposite each other.

**Floor Bridge:** Lie down on your back with your knees bent, feet flat on the floor. Rest your arms at your sides, palms down. Draw your belly in and push through your heels to lift your pelvis off the floor. Slowly lower your hips and pelvis back to the floor.

**Leg Crab Kick:** Get into a crab walk position by lying on your back and extending your arms and your legs up so you are supporting yourself with your hands and feet. Once your bottom is in the air, kick out with your right leg. Bring the right leg back and kick out with your left leg. Alternate between legs.

**Air Jump Rope:** Jump up and down while moving your arms in a circular motion as if you were swinging a jump rope.

**Chest Touch Pushups:** Start in an elevated position with your arms holding you up. Keep your body straight, head facing forward. Lower yourself towards the ground with both arms. Once your chest touches the ground start pushing back up to your starting position, while touching the left side of your chest with your right hand. Once completed drop your right arm down to the ground so you are holding yourself up with both arms in your starting position. Repeat the exercise, this time touching the right side of your chest with your left arm. Alternate between left and right.

**Plank:** Lie face down while resting on your forearms with your feet together. Sweep the floor with your arms to separate your shoulders and tuck your chin, creating a straight line from the top of your head to your heels. Hold this position.

**Side Step:** Lunge out to your right. Back leg straight, bend the right knee. Slide back and bend the left knee and straighten the right leg. Turn and face the opposite direction and repeat.

**Mountain Climbers:** Start in your pushup position. Then lift one leg a few inches off the ground and pull it up towards your chest. Hold your knee tucked in for 2 seconds, then return to your start position. Alternate legs like you are climbing up a mountain.

**Toe Taps:** Start by standing with your two feet shoulder length apart with your back straight and your arms by your sides. While jumping straight up, bring one toe forward to the front and tap while alternating to the opposite foot. Go back and forth between your left and right foot. Find a rhythm and be careful not to lose your balance!

# NUTRITION

Hey Parents!

A healthy diet and daily exercise will maximize the likelihood of your child growing up healthy and strong. Children are constantly growing and adding bone and muscle mass, so a balanced diet is very important to their overall health. Try to provide three nutritious meals a day that all include fruits and vegetables. Try to limit fast food and cook at home as often as you can. Not only is it better on your pocketbook, cooking at home is better for you and can be done together as a family. Everyone can help and it is more likely you will eat together as a family.

As a healthy eating goal, avoid food and drinks that are high in sugar as much as possible. Provide fresh fruits, vegetables, grains, lean meats, chicken, fish and low-fat dairy items as much as possible.

## 5 Steps to Improve Eating Habits

 Make fresh fruits and vegetables readily available

 Cook more at home, and sit down for dinner as a family

 Limit sugary drinks, cereals and desserts

 Serve smaller portions

 Limit snacks to 1 or 2 daily

# HEALTHY EATING POP QUIZ!

## What does eating healthy mean to you?

List your 3 favorite healthy foods:

1) _____    2) _____    3) _____

If you were only to eat vegetables,
what 5 vegetables would you choose?

1) _____    2) _____

3) _____    4) _____    5) _____

Fill in the names of 5 different food groups on the Food Plate.

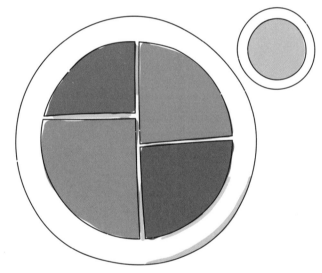

Circle the food and drink items that are healthy foods from the list below:

| | | | |
|---|---|---|---|
| *Milk* | *Apple* | *Chicken* | *Salad* |
| *candy* | *butter* | *soda* | *orange* |
| *ice cream* | *carrot* | *cotton candy* | *chocolate shake* |

List your 3 favorite healthy foods

1) _____    2) _____    3) _____

Create a list of foods you would like to grow in a garden:

4-5 • © Summer Fit Activities™

# Nutrition – *Food Plate*

It is important to eat different foods from the 5 different food groups. Eating a variety of foods helps you stay healthy. Some foods give you protein and fats. Other foods give you vitamins, minerals and carbohydrates. Your body needs all of these to grow healthy and strong!

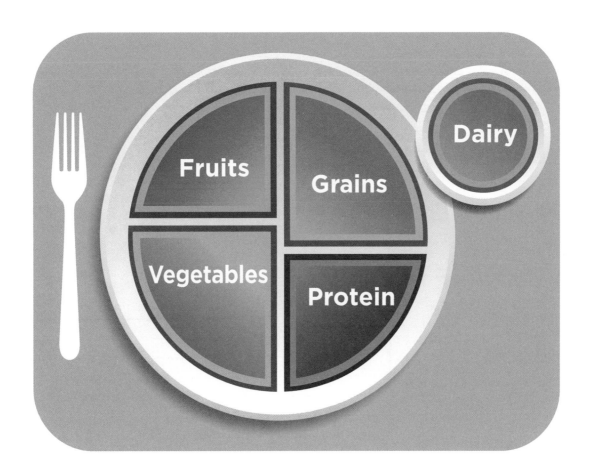

## List 3 different foods for each category.

| Fruits | Vegetables | Grains | Protein | Dairy |
|--------|-----------|--------|---------|-------|
| 1) _____ | 1) _____ | 1) _____ | 1) _____ | 1) _____ |
| 2) _____ | 2) _____ | 2) _____ | 2) _____ | 2) _____ |
| 3) _____ | 3) _____ | 3) _____ | 3) _____ | 3) _____ |

# Nutrition – *Meal Planner*

Plan out 3 balanced meals for one day.
Organize your meals so you will eat all the
recommended foods listed on the Food Plate.

**BREAKFAST**

**LUNCH**

**DINNER**

4-5 • © Summer Fit Activities™

# Nutrition – *Meal Tracker*

Use these charts to list the different foods from the different
food categories on My Plate that you eat each day.
Every day you mark each food category color in the vegetable!

| | Grains | Dairy | Protein | Fruits | Vegetables | |
|---|---|---|---|---|---|---|
| Monday | | | | | | |
| Tuesday | | | | | | |
| Wednesday | | | | | | |
| Thursday | | | | | | |
| Friday | | | | | | |
| Saturday | | | | | | |
| Sunday | | | | | | |

| | Grains | Dairy | Protein | Fruits | Vegetables | |
|---|---|---|---|---|---|---|
| Monday | | | | | | |
| Tuesday | | | | | | |
| Wednesday | | | | | | |
| Thursday | | | | | | |
| Friday | | | | | | |
| Saturday | | | | | | |
| Sunday | | | | | | |

4-5 • © Summer Fit Activities™

# MY OWN HEALTHY SNACKS

## Frozen Banana Slices

**Prep Time:** 10 minutes

**Freezer Time:** 2 hours

**Yield:** 2 servings, Good for all ages!

**Ingredients:** 2 fresh bananas

**Directions:** Peel the bananas and cut them into 5-6 slices each. Place the banana slices on a plate and place in freezer for 2 hours. Enjoy your frozen banana snack on a hot summer day!

## Yogurt Parfaits

**Prep Time:** 15 minutes

**Cook Time:** 0 minutes

**Yield:** 4 servings, Good for all ages!

**Ingredients:** 2 cups fresh fruit, at least 2 different kinds (can also be thawed fresh fruit)
1 cup low-fat plain or soy yogurt
4 TBSP 100% fruit spread
1 cup granola or dry cereal

**Directions:** Wash and cut fruit into small pieces. In a bowl, mix the yogurt and fruit spread together. Layer each of the four parfaits as follows: Fruit Yogurt Granola (repeat) Enjoy!

## Frozen Grapes

**Prep Time:** 10 minutes

**Freezer Time:** 2 hours

**Yield:** 4 servings, Good for all ages!

**Ingredients:** Seedless grapes

**Directions:** Wash seedless grapes and separate them from their stem. Place into a bowl or plastic bag. Put them into the freezer for 2 hours. Enjoy your cold, sweet and crunchy treat!

## Fruit Smoothies

**Prep Time:** 5 minutes

**Cook Time:** 0 minutes

**Yield:** 2 servings, Good for all ages!

**Ingredients:** 1 cup berries, fresh or frozen
4 ounces Greek yogurt
1/2 cup 100% apple juice
1 banana, cut into chunks
4 ice cubes

**Directions:** Place apple juice, yogurt, berries and banana into blender. Cover and blend until smooth. While the blender is running, drop ice cubes into the blender one at a time. Blend until smooth. Pour and enjoy!

4-5 • © Summer Fit Activities"

| Alabama | Alaska | Arizona | Arkansas |
|---|---|---|---|
| Montgomery | Juneau | Phoenix | Little Rock |
| California | Colorado | Connecticut | Delaware |
| Sacramento | Denver | Hartford | Dover |
| Florida | Georgia | Hawaii | Idaho |
| Tallahassee | Atlanta | Honolulu | Boise |

A

| Illinois | Indiana | Iowa | Kansas |
|---|---|---|---|
| Springfield | Indianapolis | Des Moines | Topeka |

| Kentucky | Louisiana | Maine | Maryland |
|---|---|---|---|
| Frankfort | Baton Rouge | Augusta | Annapolis |

| Massachusetts | Michigan | Minnesota | Mississippi |
|---|---|---|---|
| Boston | Lansing | Saint Paul | Jackson |

B

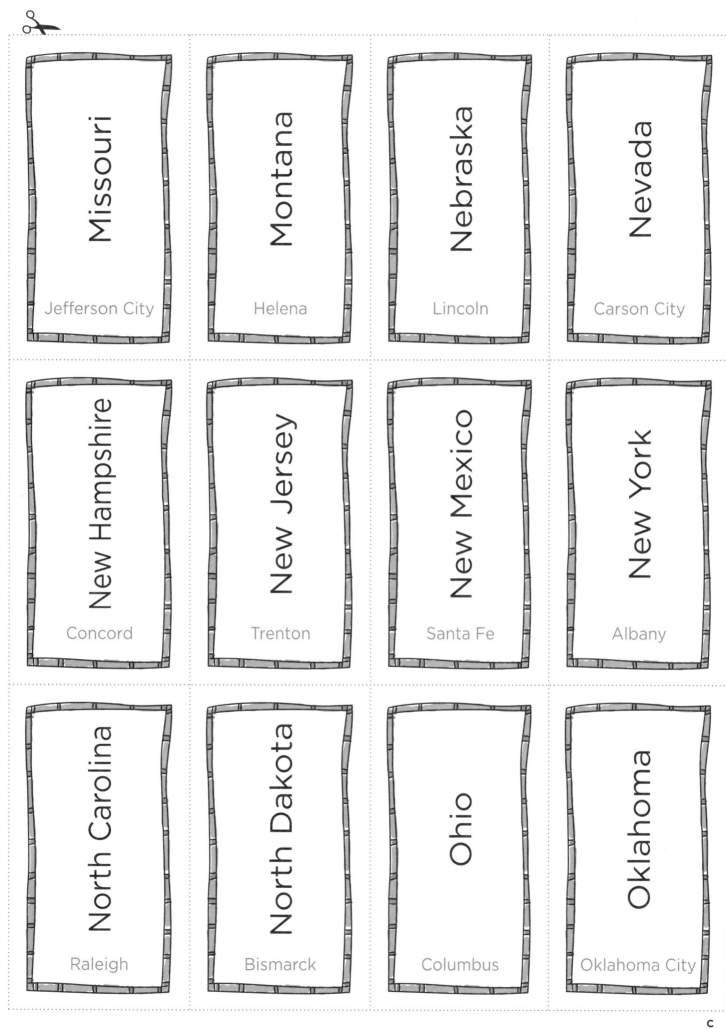

Missouri

Jefferson City

Montana

Helena

Nebraska

Lincoln

Nevada

Carson City

New Hampshire

Concord

New Jersey

Trenton

New Mexico

Santa Fe

New York

Albany

North Carolina

Raleigh

North Dakota

Bismarck

Ohio

Columbus

Oklahoma

Oklahoma City

| Oregon | Pennsylvania | Rhode Island | South Carolina |
|--------|-------------|--------------|----------------|
| Salem | Harrisburg | Providence | Columbia |
| South Dakota | Tennessee | Texas | Utah |
| Pierre | Nashville | Austin | Salt Lake City |
| Vermont | Virginia | Washington | West Virginia |
| Montpelier | Richmond | Olympia | Charleston |

D

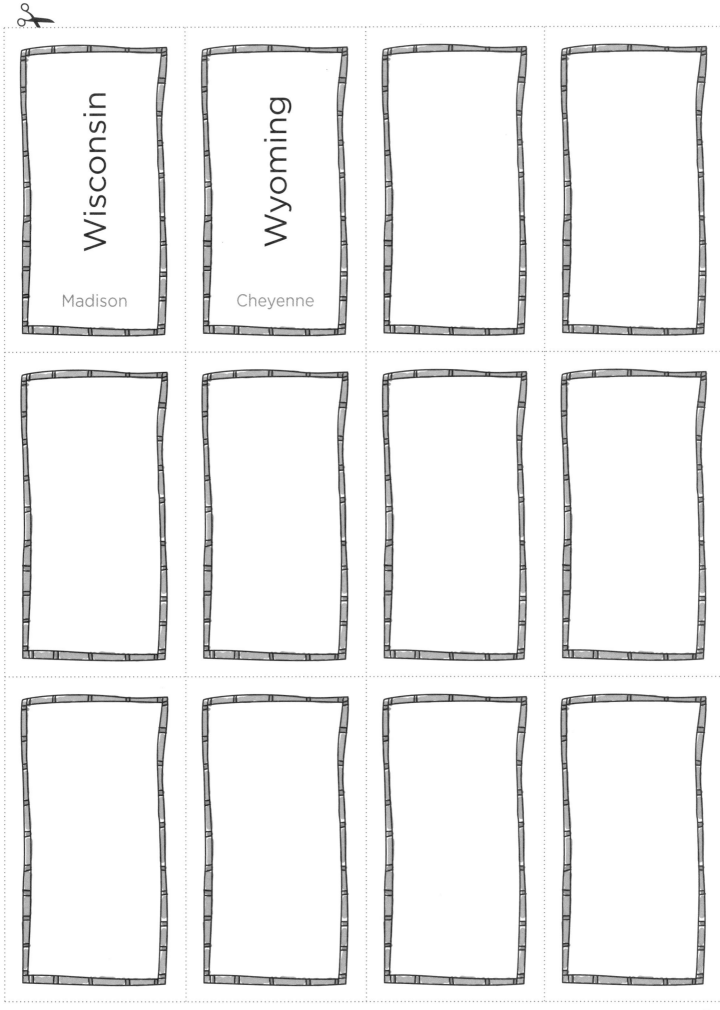

Wisconsin

Madison

Wyoming

Cheyenne

E

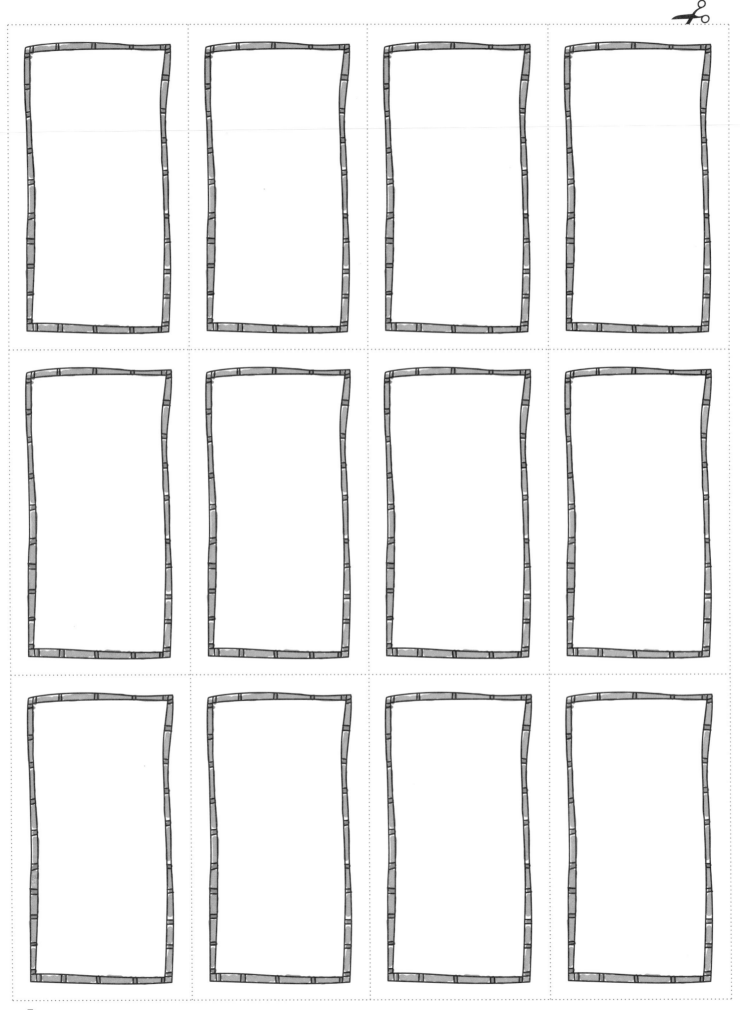

F

utensil

mortal

vocal

mental

whine

measure

remember

early

hours

twenty

products

happened

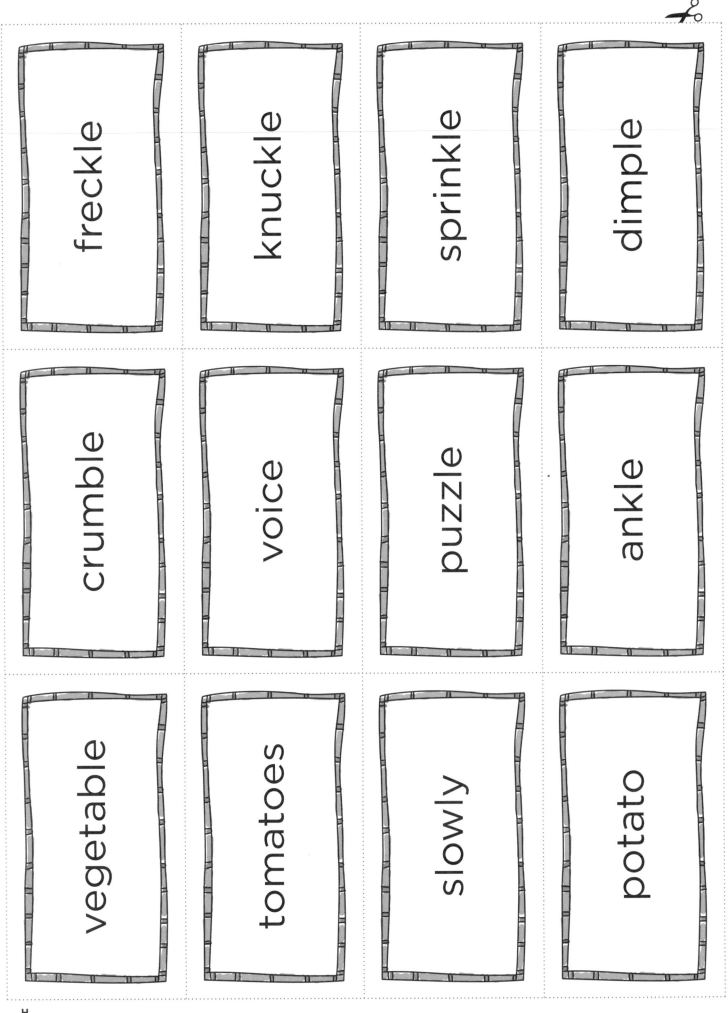

| freckle | crumble | vegetable |
| knuckle | voice | tomatoes |
| sprinkle | puzzle | slowly |
| dimple | ankle | potato |

H

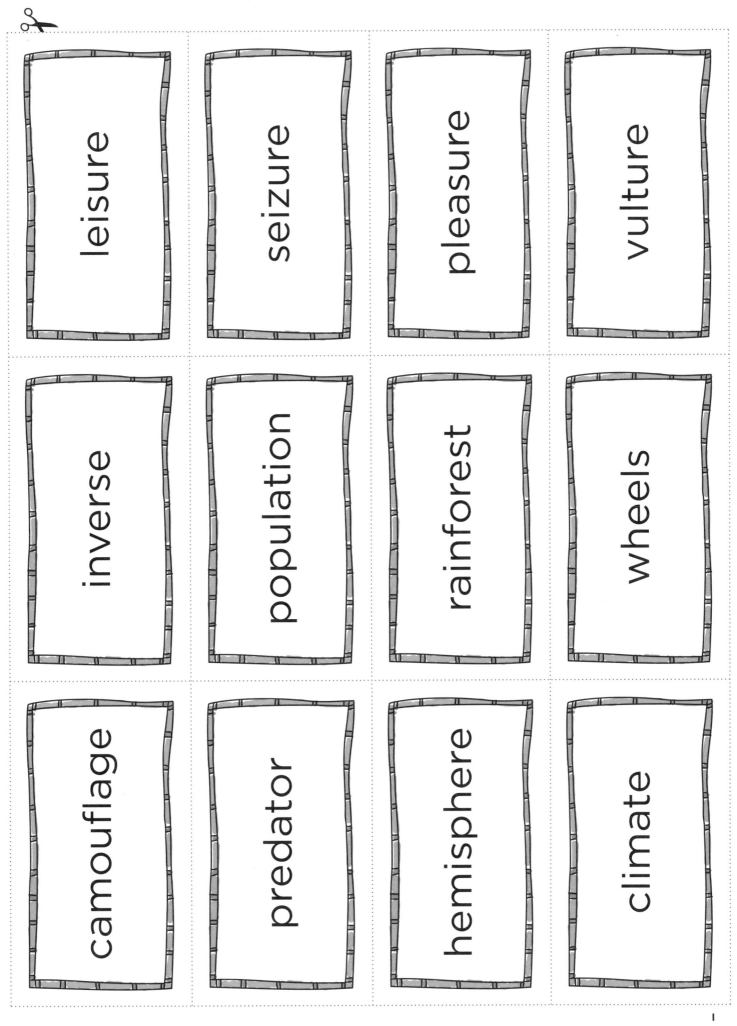

leisure

seizure

pleasure

vulture

inverse

population

rainforest

wheels

camouflage

predator

hemisphere

climate

1

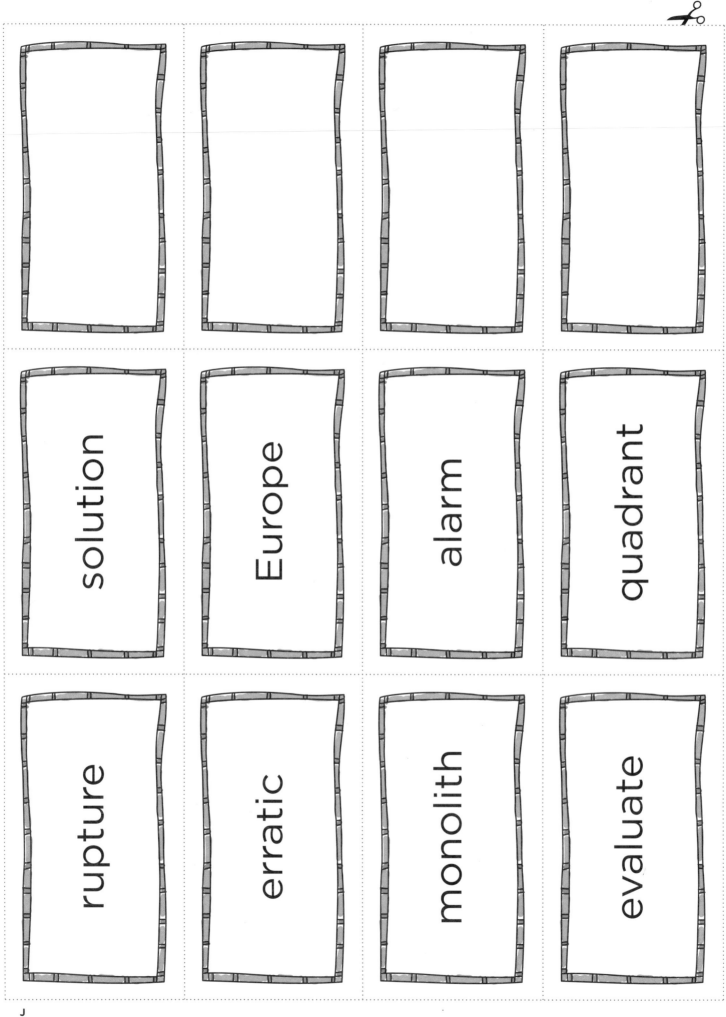

rupture

erratic

monolith

evaluate

solution

Europe

alarm

quadrant

J

Value of **Curiosity**

Value of **Humor**

Value of **Love**

Value of **Kindness**

Value of **Dedication**

Value of **Friendship**

Value of **Giving**

Value of **Saving**

Value of **Understanding**

Value of **Imagination**

Value of **Responsibility**

Value of **Helping**

K

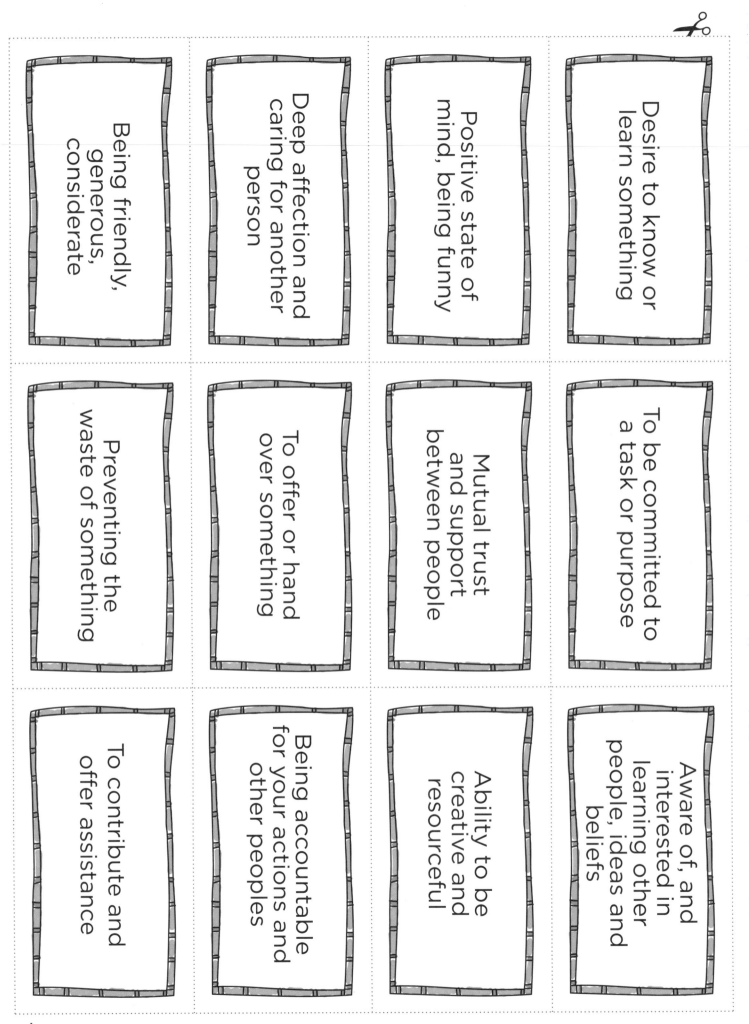

Being friendly, generous, considerate

Deep affection and caring for another person

Positive state of mind, being funny

Desire to know or learn something

Preventing the waste of something

To offer or hand over something

Mutual trust and support between people

To be committed to a task or purpose

To contribute and offer assistance

Being accountable for your actions and other peoples

Ability to be creative and resourceful

Aware of, and interested in learning other people, ideas and beliefs

L

Value of **Truth**

Value of **Belief**

Value of **Respect**

Value of **Courage**

Value of **Honesty**

Value of **Sharing**

Value of **Patience**

Value of **Determination**

Value of **Caring**

Value of **Foresight**

Value of **Learning**

Value of **Fantasy**

M

A fact, belief or person that is accepted as being true

Trust, faith or confidence in someone or something

Admire someone for their abilities, qualities or achievements

Ability to do something that frightens you

Sincere, free of deceit

To give to others

Accept or tolerate without getting upset

Being resolute to an idea or purpose

Displaying kindness and concern for others

Being able to predict needs or what will happen in the future

Knowledge through experience, study or being taught

Being able to imagine the impossible

# CERTIFICATE OF COMPLETION

## Summer Fit Activities

Has Completed

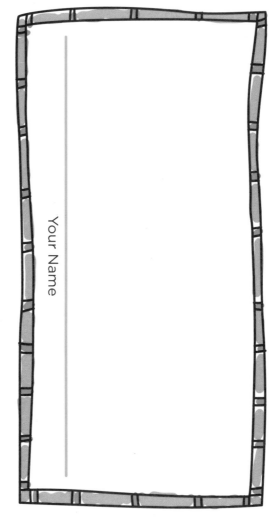

Your Name

_____
Parent Signature

SummerFitActivities.com

Summer Fit Activities
Published by Active Planet Kids